THE
PARAS
THE STORY OF THE PARACHUTE REGIMENT

THE PARAS

THE STORY OF THE PARACHUTE REGIMENT

Theodore Rowland-Entwistle

PARRAGON

First published in Great Britain in 1997 by

Parragon

Unit 13–17

Avonbridge Trading Estate

Atlantic Road

Avonmouth

Bristol BS11 9QD

Copyright © Parragon 1997

ISBN: 0-7525-2235-3

Conceived, designed and produced by Haldane Mason, London

ACKNOWLEDGEMENTS
Art Director: Ron Samuels
Editor: Tessa Rose
Designers: Ron Samuels/David Robinson
Picture Research: Tessa Rose/Charles Dixon-Spain
Indexer: Conan Nicholas

Colour reproduction by Regent Publishing Services, Hong Kong

Printed in Italy

Picture Acknowledgements:

All photographs were supplied courtesy of the Airborne Forces Museum, Aldershot, except for those on the following pages which are from the Military Picture Library, Aldershot: Front cover, back cover, pages 1, 2/3, 6/7, 16, 72/73, 89, 92; and those on page 18–19 which are copyright the Red Devils.

Author's Acknowledgement:

I would like to express my thanks for the help and encouragement I received from Dave Brown, secretary of the Hastings Branch of the Parachute Regimental Association, and his comrades.

Page 1: Parachute Jumping Instructors dispatch troops from 2 Para over Imber DZ (Drop Zone).
Page 2–3: A pathfinder from 5 Airbourne Brigade in free fall at the moment his barometrically opened GQ360 parachute deploys at a height of about 400 m (1200 ft).
Page 5: Since their inception in the Second World War the Parachute Regiment has fulfilled many roles all over the world.
Page 6–7: Armed with SA80 rifles, the men of 2 Para on charge while on exercise.
Page 8–9: Over Ranville DZ in Normandy, the paras perform a huge low level operation to mark the 50th anniversary of D-Day.

CONTENTS

WHO ARE THE PARAS?

Well, who are they? First and foremost, they are soldiers, part of the PBI (Poor Bloody Infantry), the people who in the long run win battles and, ultimately, wars. Like the Special Air Service (the SAS) and the Royal Marine Commandos, they are an élite group. They are volunteers in the British Army, and highly trained to be in the forefront of any attack.

And they have their own special method of leading an attack: literally, they often leap into action, floating to the ground on parachutes, often under a storm of fire.

Their official title is the Parachute Regiment. The regiment has three regular battalions: 1 Para, 2 Para, and 3 Para. It has its headquarters at Aldershot in Hampshire, which has been an army town since 1854 with two camps, north and south.

The Paras' training and their courage have set them in the vanguard wherever there is trouble. The regiment was created in the heat of World War II, when Britain found itself alone against the apparently invincible might of Nazi Germany. Since then the Paras have played their part in most of the small wars which Britain has fought while Europe itself has mainly been at

peace: Palestine, Cyprus, Suez, Aden, Borneo, and the Falklands.

Training is rigorous, and many volunteers cannot make the grade, which demands an exceptional standard of fitness, discipline, and initiative. The proudest moment of a Para is when he is judged fit to receive the prized red beret which is the hallmark of the regiment. The beret and its colour were decided on in 1942 by Major General Frederick 'Boy' Browning, then commanding 1st Airborne Division. Tradition has it that several colours were tried for the beret, and the final choice was made by the soldier who was modelling the various colours in front of the Chief of the Imperial General Staff, General Sir Alan Brooke, who had been unable to come to a decision himself. It was probably the colour of the berets as well as the fighting spirit of the Paras that prompted their German opponents in North Africa to describe them as 'Rote Teufel' – Red Devils. And the Red Devils they have been known as ever since.

The emblem of the Airborne Forces, showing the mythical Greek warrior Bellerophon astride his equally fabulous winged horse, Pegasus, was designed and adopted at the same time.

Men of 2 Para, wearing their prized red berets, sprint through a cloud of dense smoke as they attack a position. They are armed with 5.6 mm L85A1 SA80 rifles and L86A1 weapons.

BIRTH OF AN ELITE

It all began on 22 June 1940, in the darkest days of World War II. A note went from Winston Churchill, the Prime Minister, to General Sir Hastings Ismay, who was the head of the military wing of the War Cabinet Secretariat. The secretariat was a link between the civilian government and the Army. Churchill wrote: 'We ought to have a corps of at least five thousand parachute troops. Advantage can be taken of the summer to train these troops, who can none the less play their part meanwhile as shock troops home defence. Pray let me have a note from the War Office on the subject.'

A CALL TO ARMS

Below: The Prime Minister Winston Churchill was instrumental in setting up the force that would become the Parachute Regiment. He saw the need for a force of at least 5,000 parachute troops and asked the Army to see to their training. Churchill is seen here during a visit to 1st Airborne Division on Salisbury Plain.

The Army responded quickly to Churchill's note to Ismay. Within two days Major John F. Rock of the Royal Engineers was ordered to take charge of organizing British airborne forces. But he was not given any orders or advice on how he was to set about the task, or who were the men to be in them. Though he had flown as a passenger in aircraft, he knew nothing about parachutes or gliders, which were to be the essentials of the force. All he, and for that matter Churchill, knew was that the Germans in their Blitzkrieg (lightning war) which had overrun the Netherlands and Belgium had used parachute troops to good advantage, and that the Russians also had a large parachute force.

Major Rock, soon promoted to the rank of lieutenant colonel, was dispatched to Ringway, Manchester's civilian airport, which was judged to be sufficiently far from the vulner-able south coast of England, where heavy air raids were imminently – and rightly – expected. Ringway was renamed the Central Landing School, and later retitled the Central Landing Establishment. There was some confusion over the name: the War Office itself was guilty of sending a letter to Rock at 'The Central Laundry', and one volunteer received a letter addressed to 'The Central Sunday School'. It was no Sunday school: Ringway was a tough place where volunteers underwent a tough and dangerous initiation into the art of leaping into action.

Rock was soon joined by officers and men from the RAF, principally two wing-commanders, Louis Strange and Sir Nigel Norman. There were men from the RAF parachute section, and some NCOs from the Army's Physical Training Corps. These men became instructors. The soldiers wore the red parachute

flashes that spoke of their work; the RAF instructors did not because, as someone at the Air Ministry put it, 'it is the duty of the RAF to remain in the air, not fall out of it'.

THE FALL OF FRANCE

When Churchill wrote that fateful memorandum to General Ismay, he had been prime minister only since 10 May. In those few weeks he and Britain had watched with horror as German troops not only overwhelmed the Netherlands and Belgium, but forced the surrender of Norway and Denmark. The Germans finally accepted the capitulation of France on the very day Churchill sent his memorandum to General Ismay.

DUNKIRK

The British Expeditionary Force, which had been fighting fiercely to repel the attacks on the Low Countries and France, retreated together with some allied troops to the beaches at Dunkirk in northern France. From there a fleet of 861 ships and boats – some of them very small boats – lifted the men off and ferried them back to England, under heavy attack from the air. More than 200 vessels in this gallant fleet were sunk, but they saved 338,226 British and Allied soldiers. The rest of the men of the British Expeditionary Force went into captivity, and all their equipment, including personal weapons, became spoils of war.

Some people hailed Dunkirk as a victory. It was not: it was a defeat, and one as heavy and crushing as the British Army had ever known. But thanks to the gallantry of a fleet of fishermen, part-time sailors, the crews of lifeboats from liners in the London docks – in fact anyone who

had a seaworthy boat – something was salvaged from the disaster. That something was not just lives, but pride. The phrase 'the Dunkirk spirit' passed into the language, and it was that spirit which enabled London and other British cities to endure the fearsome bombing raids – the Blitz – that were so soon to follow.

THE ESTABLISHMENT VIEW

The Russians had already grasped the possibilities of parachute troops. Back in 1929 they had used them to repel an Afghan invasion of the then Soviet republic of Tadjikistan. The Russians went on to make parachute jumping a national sport, and in 1936 they put on a display during their summer manoeuvres. They dropped 1,200 men plus machine-guns and light field guns.

In spite of this – and the Russian display had been witnessed by a very

Above: The German and Soviet armed forces had been quick to see the potential of parachute troops, and at the outbreak of war in 1939 a pattern of training and deployment was already established. The British, by contrast, had a lot of catching up to do. Here a group of German airborne troops is undergoing ground training.

senior British general – many people in Britain were doubtful about the use of parachute troops. The training of Britain's new force was handed over to the Royal Air Force, which at least knew how to use parachutes. But the higher-ups at the Air Ministry poured cold water on the scheme. A paper from the Air Staff on 12 August explained that there were 'difficulties', and added:

'We are beginning to incline to the view that dropping troops from the air by parachute is a clumsy and obsolescent method, and that there are far more important possibilities in gliders.

'The Germans made excellent use of their parachute troops in the Low Countries by exploiting surprise, and by virtue of the fact that they had virtually no opposition. But it seems to us that this may be the last time that parachute troops are used on a serious scale in major operations.'

It is remarkable how often the 'establishment view' turns out to be wrong. In one aspect the establishment had their way: they trimmed Churchill's proposed numbers down. After the war he wrote: 'I regret however that I allowed the scale I had proposed for British parachute troops to be reduced from five thousand to five hundred.'

However, in fairness to the RAF, 500 was as many as it was possible to train quickly with the resources and experience then available.

THE AIRBORNE DIVISIONS

The Paras were not alone in the new Army air arm that was being created. They were part of what came to be known as the Airborne Divisions. Obviously it was not going to be possible to transport large numbers of troops and large quantities of heavy, bulky weapons and supplies by parachute, though it was surprising just what could be floated down to earth under a lightweight canopy. The Air Ministry was already working on the idea of using expendable gliders, cheap to manufacture, which could be towed to a landing ground and cast off from the tow and complete their journey without power.

THE GLIDERS

The gliders were made of wood. The first model was the Hotspur, which was used largely for training. The final operational gliders of World War II were the Horsa and the Hamilcar. Each glider was made with a wooden frame covered with a plywood skin, and looked a bit like a small London Underground railway carriage fitted with a single high wing and a three-wheeled undercarriage. The Horsa was about 20

THE LION'S ROAR

Winston Leonard Spencer-Churchill was a remarkable man. At the time he became prime minister he was nearly 66, an age when most men today are already in retirement. In his long life he had been a soldier, then a Member of Parliament, and had held every high Cabinet office except prime minister. He began his political life as a Conservative, then crossed over to the Liberal Party for 20 years. For a time in World War I he returned to the Army.

When World War II began in 1939, Churchill had been a Conservative back-bencher for 10 years, at odds with his party leaders. He was constantly warning of the the dangers of the warlike Nazi Germany which its dictator, Adolf Hitler, was creating. When war began with the German invasion of Poland in September 1939, Churchill was recalled to office as First Lord of the Admiralty – the post he had held at the beginning of World War I 25 years earlier.

He proved to be the right leader for Britain in its time of peril. By hard work and his defiant wartime speeches he kept the country's spirits up. Of those speeches he said that the country was the lion; he had the honour of supplying the roar.

metres (67 feet) long, with a 27-metre (88 feet) wingspan.

One advantage of the wooden construction was that the gliders could float if they came down in the sea, and sometimes did so for as long as 24 hours. Significantly, the soldiers and crew had lifejackets but no parachutes. Each glider had two pilots, who could communicate with the pilot of the towing aircraft by means of a telephone line in the heavy towing cable, which was 107 metres (350 feet) long. Unfortunately, as the cable stretched the telephone line often broke. It was the glider pilots' responsibility to cast off the tow-rope at the appropriate moment.

The Horsa carried soldiers with their packs and weapons, and also jeeps and anti-tank guns. The Hamilcar was larger and was designed mainly for freight, such as a light tank, two Bren-gun carriers, or two jeeps with trailers. The crews rode in their vehicles. Just before landing they started the engines, so that the moment the glider landed and its nose door opened they could drive straight out and into action.

On operations the Paras landed first and prepared a landing ground, at night marking it out with flares. The gliders then flew in with reinforcements. The glider arm was finally disbanded in 1946.

Above: The Horsa glider Mark I. Cheap to build and expendable, they were towed to the landing ground and then cast off to complete their journey, unpowered, to land, where they delivered their cargo of men and light equipment.

Below: The Hamilcar was more cumbersome than the Horsa, though its basic wooden construction was similar. It was used to carry heavy equipment, such as the Tetrack light tank.

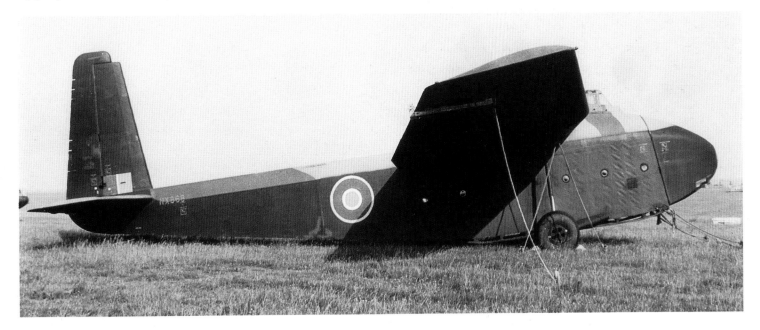

PARACHUTES

Right: It's a long way down! In this shot of a training parachute jump from a Dakota the static line attached to the aircraft can be seen at top left. This line pulls the parachute open automatically.

Below: Packing parachutes in a hanger at Ringway in 1941. The notice says it all. Most of this work was done by women, but each Para had to know how to do this job for himself in the field.

The Chinese are credited with trying out primitive parachutes as early as the 1100s, but little is known about their experiments. As with so many things, the Renaissance artist Leonardo da Vinci was the first European to design a parachute. In 1514 he drew a sketch of it in one of his many notebooks, with the following observation:

'If a man have a tent made of linen of which the apertures have all been stopped up, and it be twelve braccia across and twelve in depth, he will be able to throw himself down from any great height without sustaining any injury.'

A 'braccio' (plural 'braccia') was an ancient Italian measure more than 50 cm (20 inches) long. So Leonardo's design had dimensions not very different from those of the present-day man-carrying parachute. Like so many of Leonardo's ideas, this one never went into production.

The next person to put forward a parachute idea was Fausto Veranzio, a talented Italian priest, scientist, and inventor. In his treatise 'Machinae novae', which he published in Venice in 1595, he included a design for a parachute, along with many other mechanical devices.

THE PIONEERS

In 1783 a French chemist, Louis Sébastien Lenormand (1757–1839) made a parachute-type drop from the

tower of the Montpellier Observatory in southern France, holding a large umbrella in each hand. His is generally credited as being the first successful jump, though Hungarian and Thai athletes are reported to have made jumps in the 1600s.

The first person to experiment with a true parachute was the elder of the two Montgolfier brothers, Joseph (1740–1810) and Jacques (1745–99). They were the sons of a paper manufacturer at Annonay, in south-eastern France. They combined their knowledge of paper with a sound scientific training, and invented the first hot-air balloon. Their pioneer balloon, demonstrated in 1783, had a sphere made of paper and fabric. After Jacques died, Joseph devoted all his energies to scientific research, and produced a type of parachute in the early years of the 19th century.

The next pioneer in the world of parachutes was Jean Pierre Blanchard (1753–1809), who was born at Les Andelys, south-east of Rouen, in France. Inspired by the success of the Montgolfier brothers, he took to ballooning. In 1785 during a balloon flight in England, he dropped a dog in a basket suspended from a parachute, the first recorded successful use of a parachute. Later he tried parachuting himself, and died from injuries received in a drop in the Netherlands. The first person to make regular parachute jumps was another French balloonist, André Garnerin (1769–1823). His first attempt was in 1797, from a balloon 600 metres (2,000 ft) up.

MILITARY USE

The first person to use a parachute as a means of escape was a Polish aero-

Harness for the main parachute

Standard helmet with camouflage cover

Reserve parachute

Pack containing the Irvin LLP Mark 1 low-level parachute

Left: A Paratrooper of the Royal Horse Artillery wearing the latest Irvin LLP Mark 1 low-level parachute and harness.

Standard army boots

naut, who jumped with one from a burning balloon in 1808. However, apart from this and one or two other spectacular escapes, parachuting from balloons remained a spectator sport until the 20th century.

The first person to try jumping from a moving aeroplane was Albert Berry, an American stunt man, in 1912 at St Louis, Missouri. German pilots began using parachutes to escape from damaged aeroplanes during the last stages of World War I. From then on parachutes became commonplace equipment for airmen in Europe and North America.

PARACHUTE MATERIALS

Early parachute canopies were made of all sorts of unlikely fabrics, such as canvas. Eventually silk was chosen as the best material, because it is light and strong and can be woven into a close, airtight fabric. During World War II nylon, which is stronger and cheaper, became the standard material for the thousands of parachutes which were needed.

Man-carrying parachutes as used during the 1939–45 conflict and subsequently are circular in shape, made from about two dozen triangular panels, more for the bigger parachutes. Each panel is made of several smaller pieces, so that if a tear occurs it cannot spread far before it is stopped by a row of stitches. A stout nylon cord between each panel leads to the harness that is fastened around the user. At the top of the parachute is a pilot chute, which inflates quickly and pulls the main parachute out of the pack in which it is stored. Some packs are worn on the back; others are made to sit on.

The canopies used by the Paras are about 11 metres (35 feet) across, larger and heavier than those used by pilots escaping from damaged aircraft. The reason for the increased size is that a Para is himself heavily laden, with his pack, his personal weapons, and possibly an additional container of weapons or other gear such as signalling equipment.

The Paras use parachutes three times the size for dropping cargo, and really big loads are floated to the ground by several parachutes

PACKING AND DESCENT

Packing a parachute is a skilled art. It must be done carefully so that the

Rip cord housing

Main suspension web

parachute comes free from its pack when needed. The lines must be so arranged that they do not become tangled. Parachutes used for escape purposes or sport are opened by the wearer pulling a device called a ripcord. For the Paras, who plunge from an open door in the aircraft that is carrying them, a static line is used. This is hooked on to a fixing in the aircraft. As the line becomes taut, it automatically opens the pack and frees the pilot chute. As soon as the main chute opens, a weak link in the static line breaks to separate the Para from the aircraft.

Each parachute has steering lines by which the Para can guide his fall to some extent, by tilting the canopy or spilling air out of one side of it. The descent is at the rate of about 6 metres (20 feet) a second.

AIR BRAKES

A modern use of parachutes is as air brakes for aircraft landing at speeds that are too high for normal runways, or for the flight decks of aircraft carriers. They are also used for braking the American Space Shuttle when it returns from flights around the Earth, and were used with the command modules of the Apollo Space flights in the 1970s, to slow them for splash-down in the ocean. Rocket-powered cars attempting to break the land speed record also rely on parachutes to stop.

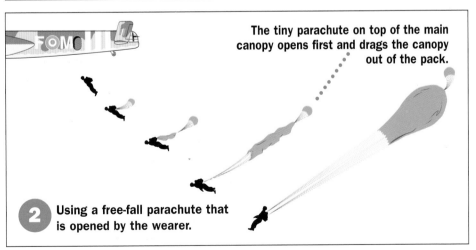

As the line becomes taut the pack opens, the pilot chute is freed and the link with the aircraft broken.

1 Using a static line parachute.

The tiny parachute on top of the main canopy opens first and drags the canopy out of the pack.

2 Using a free-fall parachute that is opened by the wearer.

Left: Static-line and free-fall parachuting. When dropped from an aircraft using a static line parachute (1), the parachutist faces away from the direction of flight and remains upright as the parachute opens. In free-fall parachuting (2), the Paratrooper faces in the direction of the flight and his attitude to the ground changes as the parachute opens.

THE RED DEVILS

The Red Devils give free-fall displays all over the world. A popular formation is the four-man star, seen here over Cyprus in 1997 (main picture). The four-man star forms part of a diamond track demonstration with two trackers (top right); once the trackers join the star, all six men will deploy their canopies (centre right). Displays with canopies involve such formations as the four-man diamond (bottom right). The beginning of another low-level display in the UK begins with a thumbs up (below).

When the Red Devils display team was formed in 1964 it was given the cumbersome name of 'The Parachute Regiment Free-Fall Team'. The present evocative name was adopted within weeks. The team's role was to improve public relations, and help to pull in new recruits. It is currently 25 strong.

At first the Red Devils used ordinary parachutes, of the type which were opened by a static line. But soon they switched to rectangular high-performance parachutes, which allow for more manoeuvrability.

Their work is a form of sport parachuting, though it has a strong training and experimental element as well. Like formation flying by aircraft, their formation jumping requires a high degree of skill, training, and constant practice. The free-fall displays begin by the team jumping out with their parachutes still firmly packed, and linking hands in the air to form a ring or

similar formation as they plummet earthward at speeds of about 190 km/h (120 mph). After some moments the parachutes are released, and the Red Devils float to the ground under control. Another popular manoeuvre is called Canopy Relative Work, in which the Red Devils link up with their canopies open, to make complicated formations in mid-air. Often the parachutists have coloured smoke canisters attached to them to make trails in the sky as they come down.

The Red Devils give about 120 displays a year, all over the world, but the income they earn has not been enough to cover their annual costs, and they receive no financial support from the Ministry of Defence. Faced with being disbanded, in 1996 the team announced that it would train civilians in the art of free-fall parachuting, with preliminary instruction on the ground, and then jumping from 3,600 m (13,000 ft) over Salisbury Plain, Wiltshire. At the end of the course the trainees, who pay a fee, are qualified to jump solo.

THE WEAPON IS FORGED

Despite the scepticism of some people at the Air Ministry, events moved quickly in creating a force of parachutists. Under Lieutenant Colonel Rock's energetic direction the work of forging the new weapon of war went ahead almost at once, and the first experimental jumps took place on 13 July, just three weeks after Winston Churchill's call for a parachute force.

The air side of training came under the experienced guidance of Lieutenant Colonel Louis A. Strange, who had served in the Royal Flying Corps (from 1918 the Royal Air Force) during World War I, when his exploits earned him the DSO, MC, and DFC. Wing Commander Sir Nigel Norman became commander of the Central Landing School. Most of the instructors came from the Physical Training Branch of the RAF, and included boxers, footballers, circus artists, film stunt men, and a ballet dancer. The parachute soldiers themselves came largely from the newly formed No. 2 Commando unit, and were all volunteers from various units of the Army.

Training at first was sketchy owing to lack of equipment, but two commercial firms rapidly made good the deficiency. An aged Whitley bomber was pressed into service. The first jumps were made by the instructors, who were also learning

their craft as they went along. They were carried out on the 'pull-off' method. The back of the rear gun turret of the bomber was removed, and the hapless pupils stood facing forwards on a tiny platform, with the twin rudders of the aircraft either side of them. At a given signal the parachutist pulled his rip cord, the parachute billowed open and he was sucked out into space by the Whitley's slipstream, to find himself floating down to earth at what seemed an incredible speed. With luck he made a safe landing. However, in the early days of training some recruits were not so lucky.

THE FIRST CASUALTIES

One man who jumped too soon missed the dropping zone, or DZ to generations of parachutists, and found himself suspended between heaven and earth from the upper branch of a large tree. Another man had his parachute blow back into the plane on top of him, and was kept in the aircraft only through the presence of mind of the instructor, who sat on him. Another man had his parachute fail to open, and was towed along through the air by the strop which attached the rip cord to the aircraft. He had a bumpy landing but was unhurt.

Several volunteers were killed, the first fatal accident occurring during the first fortnight of the training programme. Some men received severe injuries. One man, about to jump, saw on the ground far below two tiny figures carrying a stretcher with something on it, a motionless figure. But he went on to jump in his turn. That was the sort of courage needed for training in those early days, and the sort that is still needed. Even so, in the first two months two volunteers had been killed, and twenty badly injured. Not surprisingly, thirty had refused to jump. They were returned to their original army units.

THROUGH THE HOLE

As training progressed an alternative method of leaving the aircraft was devised. A hole was cut in the bottom of the Whitley's fuselage. It was a small hole, and about 1 m (3 ft) deep. The parachutist either sat, as upright as possible, with his feet over the hole, or stood to attention on the edge. This was not a matter of military drill, just that the 'attention' position was the best possible attitude

Above: A paratrooper in drop order, 1945. On operations the large pack was attached by a line, so it hit the ground first – and with luck did not burst open.

Left: A squad of volunteers lines up to board a Whitley bomber at Ringway in 1941. Compare the headgear with the later type shown in the photograph above.

Above: A volunteer making a dummy descent in one of the hangars at Ringway. Ground training such as this could be as hairy as a jump from a real aircraft and produced a crop of sprains and dislocations.

through a hole attached to a rope, which was attached to a counter-weight designed to minimize the shock of landing. The idea was to simulate the effect of landing with a parachute. It did not work, and a crop of sprains and dislocations ensured that this unpopular machine was soon abandoned. So was the practice of jumping off the back of moving lorries, which produced similar injuries. Better results were achieved by attaching the jumper to a rope wound round a large drum. As the drum revolved two large blades acted as an air-brake, rather like the governor that was fitted to an old-fashioned steam-engine.

BALLOONS TO THE RESCUE

Eventually early training was carried out by jumping from captive balloons, similar to the barrage balloons which ringed London and other vulnerable cities to try to deter enemy aircraft – and at all events to keep them from flying low. An instructor on the ground with a megaphone bellowed instructions to the novice parachutists.

Gradually the training settled into a successful routine. Within a year 40 parachutists were being trained every week and were ready for action.

Along with the training equipment other equipment was designed and tested. Among the most popular items was the 'airborne smock', a comfortable top garment which proved ideal for parachuting. Spring-heeled boots were proposed, to minimize the shock of landing, until somebody pointed out that they would be impossible to march and fight in, which was the purpose of the Paras in the first place. Other

for a clean exit. Otherwise it was possible to bang one's head on one side of the hole, or one's parachute pack on the other, neither a particularly comfortable feeling.

Lack of equipment and expertise made it essential to experiment and improvise. Since there were never enough Whitleys for all the trainees, it was necessary to devise substitutes. A device which soon acquired the nickname 'The Gallows' was rigged up in one of the huge hangars at Ringway. The recruit jumped devices were tested by dropping sandbags and other weighty objects instead of men, and the number of 'casualties' among the sandbags proved how necessary it was to do these dummy runs.

Men on the ground are no use without their equipment. So containers which could carry rifles and ammunition were designed and dropped. The cargo came through the bottom of the prototype containers, but eventually sturdy containers were constructed which could safely land mortars and Bren guns, with their ammunition. Later in the war the Paras devised a way of taking their gear with them. A bag containing up to 45 kg (100 lb) of equipment was attached by a long rope to the parachutist's waist. The bag fell ahead of the man, thus speeding his descent, which slowed when the bag hit the ground first.

THE LION ROARS AGAIN

In April 1941 a demonstration at Ringway was laid on by the Paras for the benefit of Winston Churchill. The prime minister was clearly not impressed by what he saw, or the progress that was being made. A stiff memorandum sped to General Ismay, asking for all the files relating to the reduction in numbers of Paras from 5,000 to 500. Churchill obviously felt that he had been pressured into agreeing to this reduction against his better judgement. By the time he received an adequate reply the Germans had invaded Crete (on 20 May 1941) with airborne forces, including parachute troops.

The lion roared again, but sadly. He blamed himself for following the advice of the Air Ministry staff, and added: 'A whole year has been lost, and I now invite the Chiefs of Staff to make proposals for trying, so far as is possible, to repair the misfortune.'

The result of this broadside from Churchill was that the Chiefs of Staff promised he would have his 5,000 paratroopers by May 1942, unfortunately still a year ahead.

THE NEW BROOM

To achieve this target a radical overhaul of training was needed, and a new man was brought in to take charge of it. Lieutenant Colonel Strange volunteered for a different and even more risky job: flying Hurricane fighter aircraft catapulted into the air from merchant ships.

The new man was Wing Commander Maurice Newnham, a World War I fighter pilot who had been given a desk job at Ringway in charge of administration. He determined to take the fear, and much of the risk, out of training, so that fewer of the volunteers, all picked men, would drop out (the wastage rate was about 15 per cent). He made his own first jump from a captive balloon so that he knew what it was all about, and decided that training from balloons was the ideal solution, because the ambience was quiet. The pupils could be 'talked down' by instructors with loudhailers. As a result he got everyone to believe that parachuting was a normal, almost an everyday, activity. Injuries decreased, training speeded up, and the 5,000 target seemed well within grasp.

THE WEAPON IS TESTED

Meanwhile the new weapon had received its first test. Italy, which had entered the war in the wake of the German occupation of France, seemed a likely place for a raid. The target chosen was the Tragino Aqueduct, which carried the water supply for the whole province of Apulia and its population of 2,000,000. The province also had many factories, and the ports of Bari, Brindisi, and Taranto. From them Benito Mussolini, the Italian Fascist dictator, was dispatching troops to North Africa, where they were trying to conquer Egypt, and to Albania, which Mussolini was aiming to annex. A water shortage, even if only temporary, seemed likely to hamper the Italians considerably. Bombing had been considered, but with the equipment and techniques then available the chances of hitting the target were slim.

OPERATION COLOSSUS

So Operation Colossus was born. The plan was to drop a parachute force of seven officers and 31 other ranks to blow up one of the pillars of the aqueduct, and then make their way to the coast where they would be picked up by a submarine. When volunteers were called for, a long queue formed

of men burning to get into action at last. Among them were two Italians, anti-Fascists serving with the British forces and eager to do anything to free Italy from Mussolini's régime. They were to act as interpreters. One of them, Fortunato Picchi, had been the banqueting manager at the Savoy Hotel in London.

The commander of this small force was Major T. A. C. Pritchard, of the Royal Welch Fusiliers. Some of the force were to act as a covering party for the demolition team, which consisted of seven Royal Engineers led by Captain C. K. F. Daly. Also in the force was Lieutenant Antony J. Deane-Drummond. He flew ahead of the rest of the party to Malta to make all the preparations for the raid, which was to start from that island. He travelled in a Sunderland flying-boat and took with him the explosives and other gear, which were too heavy and bulky for the much smaller Whitley bombers to carry.

REHEARSALS IN ENGLAND

The Army built a brick mock-up of part of the aqueduct so that the men could practise what they were to do on the raid. The rehearsals were marked by tragedy and comedy. One man parachuted into a pond, and

The objective of the first airborne raid, codenamed Operation Colossus – Tragino Aqueduct in Italy. This photograph was used to plan the raid and to build a mock-up for the troops to practise on. When the small force reached their real objective, they discovered not the brick-built structure they had expected, but one made of reinforced concrete.

Below: A crew of a Whitley bomber at Ringway at the time of the Tragino raid. Eight Whitleys were involved in the operation: two bombed a nearby town as a diversionary tactic while the other aircraft delivered the raiding party with their equipment to the target area.

Opposite: Bruneval Radar Station, near Le Havre – the objective of Major Frost's parachute raid in February 1942.

drowned. A few days later several others were blown into tall trees, and had to be rescued by the local fire brigade.

The eight antiquated Whitley bombers which were to take part in the raid flew the party, called X-Troop, out to Malta. They flew high over German-occupied France to avoid detection, so high that they were bitterly cold, and so crowded that if anyone moved about the pilot had to be warned so that he could adjust the trim.

MOONLIGHT AND SNOW

Conditions were ideal for the raid, with bright moonlight illuminating a snow-covered landscape. Six of the Whitleys carried the raiders, one officer and five other ranks in each aircraft, while the other two were to bomb the nearby city of Foggia, which had military airfields, as a diversion. Five of the Whitleys dropped their men reasonably close to the target area, though two of them were unable to drop their containers of weapons and explosives because the release mechanism had iced up. The sixth Whitley lost its way, and eventually dropped its parachutists in the wrong valley. This was unfortunate, because the parachutists on board were the main demolition party, Captain Daly and five of his Royal Engineers.

The first task of Major Pritchard and his colleagues who had landed near the aqueduct was to find and bring in all the containers of weapons and explosives. To do this Pritchard commandeered the services of a dozen Italian farm workers

whom they found in a nearby house. The Italians were quite happy to collaborate, one saying that nothing ever happened in that area: he was obviously delighted to take part in a real adventure. The team found only part of the explosives. Pritchard detailed a junior R.E. officer, Second-Lieutenant G. W. Paterson, and the only other sapper (engineer), a sergeant, to form an emergency demolition party in the absence of Captain Daly and his men.

Paterson found to his dismay that instead of being built of brick, as he had expected, the piers of the aqueduct were made of reinforced concrete, which was much more difficult to destroy. However, he was able to blow up one of the smaller piers, plus a small bridge near by. Water poured out of the shattered aqueduct, flooding the ravine over which it passed.

ESCAPE AND CAPTURE

It was time to go. Pritchard had to abandon one parachutist, who had a broken leg, and left him in the care of a local farmer. The rendezvous was at the mouth of the River Sele, where the men expected to find a submarine waiting for them. But they never got there. Pritchard's party was surrounded by a group of women and children, and could not bring themselves to fight their way out. They surrendered. Daly and his men, who heard the explosions and realized that there was nothing left for them to do, also made for the coast, but were intercepted by police and soldiers, and had to surrender, too. The whole party ended up in a prisoner-of-war camp, with the exception of Picchi, who was questioned and shot. His fellow Italian had false papers

THE BIRTH OF RADAR

Radar stands for RAdio Detection And Ranging. It works by sending radio waves toward an object, and measuring the time taken for the waves to bounce off an object and return. The first experiments took place in 1925, and development took place rapidly in the 1930s. By the time World War II started in September 1939, Britain, Germany, and the United States had working radar stations in operation.

Britain had a chain of radar stations along its east and south coasts, ready for an attack. They proved invaluable during the Battle of Britain and the heavy bombing raids of late 1940 and early 1941. Radar was later used in night fighters, planes which stalked enemy raiders in the dark.

In case the Germans did not have airborne radar, the British adopted a plan of deception. One night-fighter pilot, named Cunningham, was particularly successful, and became known as 'Cat's Eyes' Cunningham. The story was put about that he had exceptional night vision, aided by eating quantities of carrots. The story made carrots popular, but did little to improve most people's night vision.

and a Cockney accent, and thus was not detected.

As luck would have it, there was no submarine anyway. One of the two bomb-carrying Whitleys got into difficulties, and made a forced landing near the mouth of the River Sele. Unfortunately the pilot radioed a message to that effect to Malta, not knowing of the submarine rendezvous. Reluctantly the authorities decided not to risk sending a valuable submarine and its crew into an area which would be crawling with suspicious Italians, and cancelled the relief expedition. Deane-Drummond later escaped from captivity, and reached Switzerland. From there the French Resistance guided him through France, and he then made his way to Gibraltar and flew home.

Below: Infantry support arriving on Bruneval beach to cover the withdrawal of C Company, 2 Para, after the raid on the radar base.

1 PARA IS FORMED

At the end of 1941 the Airborne Forces were taking shape. The glider arm of what was to become the 6th Airborne Division was being formed, and Major-General Frederick A. M. ('Boy') Browning was appointed to the command of the division. He was a World War I veteran and, incidentally, the husband of the novelist Daphne du Maurier. At about the same time the First Parachute Brigade (1 Para) was formed, under the command of Brigadier Richard Gale, another veteran of World War I. Soon Gale formed two more battalions, 2 Para and 3 Para, who began training hard.

Early in 1942 it became necessary to find out what apparatus the Germans were using in their chain of radar posts along the western coast of Europe. Gale selected 2 Para, rather than the now veteran 1 Para, for the task, to demonstrate that all his men were ready for action. 2 Para's commander chose C Company to carry out the raid. It was composed entirely of Scots, and was naturally known as Jock Company. Major John Frost, the adjutant of 2 Para, was picked to lead the raid. The target was a radar base in France near the little village of Bruneval, which was not far from Le Havre.

The parachutists consisted of six officers and 113 other ranks, and they were dropped in three groups. One party seized a beach, from where the Navy was to take the raiders off. Another, led by Frost, attacked a house near the radar post, where its crew were thought to be living. The third attacked the radar post itself. Frost arranged that as soon as he arrived at the door of the house he would blow a whistle as a signal for the Paras to begin the attack.

'What will you do if the door is locked?' he was asked.

'Ring the bell,' said Frost. As it happened, he didn't need to: the door was open. The raid went like clockwork: Frost and his men killed or captured all the Germans in the house, while at the radar station an expert radio engineer, Flight Sergeant E. W. F. Cox, carefully dismantled the apparatus, taking all the important parts with him. The raiders then retreated to the beach, which had been captured after a brisk fire-fight, and were taken off by naval landing craft.

The raiders lost one man killed, seven wounded, and seven who had become detached from the rest of the group and had to be left behind. They became prisoners of war.

Below: Major John Frost (in helmet), adjutant of 2 Para and leader of the daring Bruneval raid, after the operation.

NORTH AFRICA, 1942–43

The United States entered World War II in December 1941, when Japan attacked the US base at Pearl Harbor, Hawaii, and Germany and Italy promptly declared war on the USA. Churchill and the US president, Franklin D. Roosevelt, decided to settle with Germany ahead of Japan. An attack on mainland Europe was not yet possible, but an attack on the German occupying forces in French North Africa was. Operation Torch was born, a joint US-British assault under an American commander, Lieutenant General Dwight D. Eisenhower.

It was decided to use airborne forces in the campaign, and the 2nd Battalion, 503rd US Parachute Infantry, already based in Britain under the command of the British 1st Airborne Division, was chosen for the task. 'Boy' Browning insisted that this was an insufficient force, and so 1 Para was added; it had to be brought up to operational strength with men and equipment from 2 Para. The objective of the airborne forces was the capture of northern Tunisia, as part of a joint US–British air and sea assault on the Mediterranean coast. This operation was where the Paras earned their nickname of the 'Red Devils'. Another, seaborne, attack was to be made by a US force on the Atlantic coast of French West Africa.

At the same time as Operation Torch the British 8th Army, under the command of General Bernard Montgomery, finally defeated the combined German and Italian forces in Egypt and Libya and drove inexorably westward to link up with Torch. The Battle of El Alamein, which broke the German–Italian armies, began on 23 October 1942 and lasted until 6 November, by which time the 8th Army was storming across the Western Desert. Two

Below: A practice drop from a Dakota. Few Paras had experience of jumping from this type of aircraft before the North African campaign, a joint Anglo-US effort, and many learnt the hard way during the run-up to the attack.

days later Operation Torch began.

There were political complications in the North African campaign. After the fall of France in 1940, the Germans had occupied the northern part of the country, leaving the southeast under French rule, with its capital at Vichy. Vichy France, as it was known, was far from independent, but it was free from German occupation. Its ruler was the aged soldier Marshal Philippe Pétain, a hero of World War I who had been dragged out of retirement at the age of 84 to try to save France. Pétain became a collaborator with the Germans, though age, illness, and senility meant that he was a tool in the hands of the real collaborators, who included his prime minister, Pierre Laval.

French North Africa was under the control of Vichy. It was uncertain how

the French administrators in North Africa would react, nor how the indigenous population of Arabs and Berbers would regard the invasion. The German reaction was more predictable: the moment Eisenhower's forces landed the Germans occupied Vichy France.

PREPARATION

The US Army Air Force undertook to airlift the British Paras into battle, using Dakota bombers. Exit from these aircraft was through a side door, instead of through the 'hole' as in the Whitleys, and a hurried retraining was organized. Four men were killed in the initial stages until the Paras and the US pilots worked out how to cope, one problem being that the static line used by the British was too short for the

Above: A camouflaged Para manning a Vickers medium machine-gun in North Africa, 1942.

American aircraft. As it was, many of the Paras were sent off to North Africa with no experience of dropping from Dakotas. Most of them travelled by sea to Algiers, because there were not enough planes to fly them there. They left Britain on 29 October. About two-thirds of 3 Para was held back to form the initial attack, and these troops were flown to Gibraltar, landing there at dawn on 10 November.

BONE AIRFIELD

On arrival in Gibraltar the commander of 3 Para, Lieutenant Colonel Geoffrey Pine-Coffin, was told that his men were to be dropped in Algeria next day, the objective being the airfield at Bone. This port was on the border between Algeria and Tunisia. The actual attack was delivered early on the morning of 12 November, from an airfield near Algiers which was already in Allied hands.

The drop was successful, two companies of 3 Para plus their headquarters and a mortar platoon landing in or near the airport. The ground was very hard and several men suffered broken legs on landing. The Paras reached Bone just ahead of a German parachute detachment bound on the same errand. Seeing the British already there, the Germans turned back. The Paras were quickly reinforced by No. 6 Commando, who landed at Bone from the sea. They held the airfield for a week, despite heavy dive-bombing, and were then withdrawn.

BLUFF

Meanwhile, 1 and 2 Para and the rest of 3 Para landed at Algiers. A few days later 525 men of 1 Para, under Lieutenant Colonel James Hill, dropped at Souk el Arba, a road junction town east of Bone, and at once advanced on their next objective, Beja, using requisitioned French vehicles.

Some 3,000 French troops held Beja. With a bold bluff Hill persuaded

Above: Men of 1st Airborne Division advance on an objective in North Africa. Their camouflage clothing and skill in hiding made them difficult targets for the German Stuka dive-bombers patrolling the skies above them.

the French to let him take over from them, and to make his force look bigger than it was marched his men twice through the town like a stage army, once wearing steel helmets, and once in their red berets. The French were so impressed that they joined forces with the Paras to fight the Germans. Hill was seriously wounded in a skirmish in which a platoon captured six German tanks and wiped out their crews. Major Alastair Pearson took over the command. In less than a fortnight of heavy fighting Pearson had been awarded the DSO and the MC for his bold leadership.

THE ADVENTURES OF 2 PARA

Lieutenant Colonel John Frost and 2 Para had to wait impatiently in reserve for some days before being thrown into action. Then, after two changes of plan and an incredible muddle, 2 Para set off for Depienne airfield, vacated by the Germans, there to form up and march to Oudna, a German-held airfield 19 km (12 miles) away, destroy the aircraft there, and then link up with 1st Army at Tunis. The last change of plan was so late that there was no time to brief the men or pick a DZ (dropping zone) from a map. 'Right,' said Frost. 'I'll pick one from the air.' He hurriedly told the pilots of the transport Dakotas where they were going, and 2 Para set off.

Frost jumped first, and the rest of 2 Para followed. The landing was scattered and there was more confusion, made worse by a bunch of Arabs who began looting the containers of equipment. The Arabs were driven off by gunfire. Frost rallied his men by blasts on a hunting horn, and they set off to the airfield. They managed

to requisition a few mule-carts, but each man had to carry about 55 kg (120 lb) over rough, hilly tracks. It was an all-night march, with a brief halt at 4.30 in the morning. Yet 2 Para had captured the airfield by 14.30. There were no aircraft to destroy, so the Paras went on to the next objective, Tunis.

They were attacked by Stuka dive-bombers, but their camouflage clothing and their skill in hiding averted casualties. German tanks displaying US 1st Army insignia captured a few paratroopers, and told the rest they were surrounded. At the same time 2 Para received a radio message from headquarters (the only one they ever did receive). It told them that the assault on Tunis had been postponed.

HEAVY CASUALTIES

Frost had no alternative but to retreat and try to link up with 1st Army, more than 50 km (30 miles) away. He picked a strong defensive position, and held it during a day of steady German attacks. When night fell he blew his hunting horn as a signal to begin the march. They had heavy casualties – 120 dead and wounded. Sadly they had to leave the

Below: Spit and polish – an airborne soldier burnishes his boots watched by a few locals during the North African campaign. Troops in action must keep themselves and their equipment clean and in good order.

wounded, guarded by one platoon, to be captured by the Germans. They marched all night, with blistered and bleeding feet, and holed up for the day at a farm surrounded by a thick cactus hedge.

Again they fought off repeated German attacks until nightfall, when, with their ammunition almost gone, they broke out. The following afternoon they reached a main road and made contact with 1st Army. They had lost 16 officers and 250 other ranks. Even by this point the struggle was not over, and there followed a further eight days of marching and fighting until they were relieved by the Coldstream Guards, and were taken back to base for a well earned rest.

Most of them had never been in action before, and their exploit says a great deal for their training and courage. It also underlines the basic principle of being a Para: to be completely self-contained, ready to fight and look after himself when he leaps into action.

However, courage cannot compensate entirely for bad planning. The attack on Oudna was mismanaged from the top, and was based on faulty intelligence. The men of 2 Para were

THE BILL

When the Parachute Brigade was finally withdrawn for a rest, it had suffered 1,700 casualties. The butcher's bill would have been heavier but for the courage of the 16th Parachute Field Ambulance. These doctors and orderlies made up surgical teams, who were dropped with the troops, and treated the wounded under fire. One team carried out 162 operations, and only one patient died. Another measure of the worth of 2 Para is the list of their battle honours: eight DSOs, 15 MCs, nine DCMs, 22 MMs, three Croix de Guerre, and one Legion d'Honneur, won in three months of fighting.

sent against a target that no longer existed, received no support, and apart from that one radio message were ignored as far as communications were concerned.

'WAHO, MUHAMMAD!'

The Allied advance had come to a halt: Tunis would not be attacked just yet. Neither would there be any more parachute assaults. Brigadier E. W. C. Flavell, commanding the Parachute Brigade in North Africa, wanted his force withdrawn to regroup and resume training, but parachutists were not required, and infantry were. The Paras were needed to plug gaps in the line of battle, and to stiffen some of the very inexperienced American troops, who had

Below and opposite: The Allies used North Africa as a springboard for their invasion of Sicily and southern Italy. Here men of 1st Airborne Division are undergoing amphibious assault training for their next major push against the Axis forces.

lost heart after suffering reverses and wanted to go home. It should be said that they were not typical of the US Army as a whole, and certainly not of the US paratroops.

From December 1942 to April 1943 the Paras fought as ordinary infantry. The conditions were appalling, as it was winter followed by early spring in Tunisia, and the soldiers had to contend with snow, sleet, rain and mud. They were reinforced by 200 men from other units, many of them anti-aircraft gunners. These men were given red berets to make them feel at home, and the Paras gave them some basic infantry training. Some of the Paras who had been taken prisoner escaped and rejoined their companies.

The 1st Parachute Brigade came successively under the command of 2nd US Corps, then 5th US Corps, and finally 19th French Corps, where they joined some French regiments and six batteries of French artillery. They took part in some very fierce fighting, and sustained heavy casualties. In nearly every engagement the Paras were heavily outnumbered by the enemy. Before one battle they were told that they were about to be attacked by ten battalions of Germans, supported by 100 tanks. That attack never happened.

About this time the Paras adopted a new battle cry, 'Waho, Muhammad!', in imitation of the typical Arab's address to his donkey. It dismayed the Germans when they heard that cry echoing through the rocky terrain.

BOLD EXPLOITS

There were many bold exploits. In one Lieutenant G. L. W. Street was visiting his advanced posts when a German jabbed a tommy gun into him and ordered him to lead a German patrol to the British battalion headquarters. Street led them instead to a Para strongpoint, and the Germans came under heavy fire. Street and the German patrol commander dived into a fold in the ground. Said Street: 'Look out! My chaps are throwing grenades at us.' The German looked, whereupon Street hit him on the head, took his weapons, and rejoined his own men.

On another occasion men of 2 and 3 Paras were trying to eject a group of

German parachutists from a wood, and ran out of grenades. A soldier sprinted back to where there were reserve supplies, grabbed a box of grenades, and walked up and down the lines of his comrades handing them out, chanting 'Chocolates, cigarettes' in the manner of cinema usherettes of the day.

There were many other examples of cool courage, like the officer who lost a leg but sat up firing his pistol at the advancing Germans until they finished him, and the corporal who charged a party of 20 Germans. He too was killed.

THE ITALIAN CAMPAIGN, 1943–44

Once North Africa had been liberated the next target for the Allied forces was Sicily, as a first step to attacking Italy. The decision for an assault on Sicily was taken by Churchill and Roosevelt at a conference at Casablanca in Morocco. This was held in January 1943, before the North African campaign had ended. The conference was attended by General Henri Giraud, who had led the French forces in North Africa, and by General Charles de Gaulle, who had organized the Free French forces in Britain.

One reason for choosing Sicily was to ease the pressure on Malta, which was being continually raided by German and Italian planes. But it left the Allies a long fight up the length of Italy.

Below: An officer of the Airborne Division gives firing orders to artillery in Italy, 1943.

Airborne landings were to be the spearhead of the attack. The 1st Parachute Brigade needed a rest after its work and losses in North Africa; the 2nd and 3rd Brigades, back in Britain, were under strength because they had been plundered to make good the losses in the 1st Brigade. Recruiting was difficult, for only the very best soldiers could be considered, and other regiments were reluctant to let their top men volunteer. But the brigades were brought up to strength again in time for the campaign in Sicily.

The 4th Brigade was formed in the Middle East, with 156 Battalion as its core. This battalion was originally raised in India from British troops. The number of 156 Para was chosen to confuse the enemy. The 4th Brigade also included 10 Para and 11 Para. The men of 156 Para wore Australian bush hats, and grumbled when ordered to wear red berets instead. Most of the 4th Brigade were flown to Tunisia, where they joined the 1st and 2nd Brigades in the 1st Airborne Division, which also included gliders; 11 Para was left in Palestine to carry out mopping-up operations.

DROPPING INTO SICILY

The North African campaign finally ended on 13 May. Operation Husky, the Sicilian campaign, was timed to start in July. It was commanded by General Sir Harold Alexander, who had been the commander-in-chief in Egypt over Montgomery and was now deputy to Eisenhower. There were two task forces for the invasion: Montgomery and his 8th Army on the east, and General George Patton and the US 7th Army on the west. The 1st Airborne Division came under the command of Montgomery.

The Paras had two objectives: the 1st Parachute Brigade, consisting of 1, 2 and 3 Para battalions, was to take the Primasole Bridge over the River Simeto, about 13 km (8 miles) south of Catania, and the 2nd Parachute Brigade was to seize the port of Augusta and a road bridge near it. 1st Airlanding Brigade – the glider-borne force – was to capture the port of Syracuse and an important bridge near it.

Most of 1 Para, led by Lieutenant Colonel Alastair Pearson, dropped at 22.30 on 9 July, and by 2.15 the next morning 50 men had secured Primasole Bridge. They were soon reinforced by three anti-tank guns, landed by glider. The men of 2 Para were scattered, but the small force that could be gathered, 170 men, soon secured its objective, high ground to the south of the bridge.

Most of 3 Para were dropped a long way from their DZ, but some managed to make their way to the bridge in small groups. The division was hampered by having only one radio set, the rest being lost somewhere in the drop.

Many of the aircraft carrying the Paras were off course, and encountered anti-aircraft fire from Allied naval vessels, so-called 'friendly fire'. Several planes were shot down or damaged, and the confusion was made worse when pilots had to take evasive action. Another problem was

Below: A map showing the Paras' operations in Sicily, 1943. The operation began on 9 July and was completed in five weeks, but with a heavy casualty list. The first landing was made on 9 July by the glider-borne troops of 1st Airlanding Brigade, with their target the port of Syracuse and a vital road-bridge near by. 1 Para's landings on 13 July were with the objective of capturing Primasole Bridge and opening the route north to Messina.

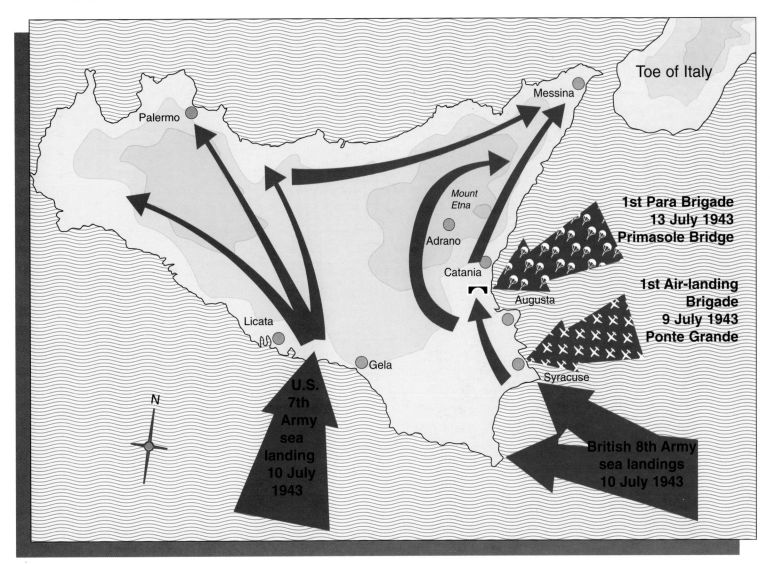

that a German parachute formation had just dropped in the same area to reinforce the Italian garrisons.

Outnumbered and outgunned, the Paras held the bridge for several hours, but eventually had to withdraw. Soon afterwards the 9th battalion of the Durham Light Infantry, part of the 4th Armoured Brigade, which had landed from the sea, arrived. The Durhams' first attack on the bridge on the morning of 15 July was beaten off with heavy casualties. A second attack was made at night, on the advice of the Paras, and the bridge was captured with few losses. Armoured Brigade transport took the battered 1 Para back to Syracuse; out of 12 officers and 280 other ranks they had 27 killed, 78 wounded, and several men missing.

THE OTHER ARM

The glider arm of the attack, commanded by Brigadier Philip Hicks, was also in trouble. It formed the spearhead of the attack, arriving on the night of 9/10 July to seize Ponte Grande near Syracuse. The force ran into bad weather, which made towing a glider especially hazardous. Many of the gliders were released too soon, and 78 plunged into the sea, some of them near the shore, others 5–6 km (3-4 miles) away. Some of the gliders floated, and those soldiers near the shore were able to swim to land. Among them was Brigadier Hicks. As he clung to the wing of his glider he murmured to his brigade-major: 'All is not well, Bill.' He and his men swam safely to shore, but 252 men were drowned.

Sixty-one gliders made it to land, mostly within 8 km (5 miles) of the Landing Zone (LZ). They landed among rocks, trees, and stone walls, but few of the troops were injured. The glider pilots sitting in the front of the aircraft were not so lucky, several being killed when their craft hit obstructions. The air-landed soldiers captured the bridge, and held it for some hours until their ammunition ran out. An hour later troops who had landed from the sea recaptured the bridge.

FRUSTRATION

Meanwhile, 2nd Parachute Brigade was standing by, ready to land and seize Augusta. To the frustration of the troops, the operation was postponed for 24 hours, and then cancelled: ground troops had already taken the port and its river bridge. The brigade was lucky, for the chosen DZ was very rocky, and there would have been heavy casualties.

From the 'inquests' after the Sicilian campaign it became clear that the operation had been badly planned, and that although the 1st Parachute Brigade had captured its objectives, and so had 1st Airlanding Brigade, the two operations had been a disaster.

For a time 1st Airborne Division was held in readiness for further parachute action, but no suitable targets were found. Instead the Paras were used as light infantry in Italy, landing at Taranto from Royal Navy warships. The Italians surrendered on 3 September 1943. As 1st Airborne arrived at Taranto they passed the Italian fleet, heading for Malta to surrender its ships. The German armies in Italy, under the command of Field Marshal Albert Kesselring, determined to continue the fight.

The 1st Parachute Brigade was held in reserve, while the 2nd and 4th brigades took part in the advance up

Italy. There followed what the official account describes as 'nine days of interesting though not very heavy fighting'; casualties in the division were fewer than 100 killed and wounded, losses which were light in the context of that war. The Paras were also used to make contact with prisoner of war camps and help the Allied prisoners to escape.

Below: Airborne 75 mm howitzers in action in the rugged landscape during the advance up the Italian 'boot'

In November 1st Parachute Brigade was sent back to England to prepare for the invasion of France. 2nd Parachute Brigade was reformed as 2nd Independent Parachute Brigade with its own supporting units, thus ensuring that the Paras would have artillery, engineers, and transport to back them up. The brigade came under the command of the 2nd New Zealand Division, and was used to hold captured areas while units of the Eighth Army continued to drive the Germans slowly back. The Paras performed this duty for four months, mostly in atrocious weather.

The Parachute brigade was also involved in the bloody battles in 1944 for Monte Cassino, a mountain 518 m (1,700 ft) high, crowned with a Benedictine monastery. It overlooks the town of Cassino and the River Rapido. The Paras spent many days holding the line, at one time in Cassino railway station with the Germans literally just across the town square. They also carried out reconnaissance and patrol work. The Cassino campaign lasted from 15 March to 18 May, at the end of which the historic monastery buildings had been reduced to rubble.

HASTY AND DRAGOON

As the Germans retreated slowly up Italy the Paras at last had a chance to use their parachutes. On 1 June in Operation Hasty, a force of 60 men from 6 Para, commanded by Captain L. A. Fitzroy-Smith, was dropped near Torricella, a town on the route along which the Germans were withdrawing. Their orders were to harass the enemy and try to prevent him from blowing up bridges. They harried the Germans for a week, losing two-thirds of their men in the process before withdrawing to the Allied lines.

In Operation Dragoon in August the Paras were involved in the invasion of southern France. A Pathfinder platoon was dropped in the early hours of 15 August and marked out a DZ for the rest of the brigade. Unfortunately, thick cloud masked the DZ, and some of the Paras landed up to 32 km (20 miles) away. They made their way to the DZ by various means, one officer actually catching a bus, and many of them walking across the hills. One platoon captured a brothel. Ignoring the dead Germans they found there, they set the girls – who were still in occupation – to cook them a meal before they resumed their march. Overall, opposition was very weak, and the Paras achieved all their objectives with the loss of only seven men killed and nine wounded.

Below: A Para well rugged up against the cold keeps watch at an artillery observation post in the mountains.

GREECE, 1944–45

Below: Fighters of the Greek National Popular Liberation Army, taken prisoner by 2nd Independent Airborne Brigade in 1943. The Paras had as much trouble with partisan fighters such as these as they did with the retreating Germans.

Bottom: Men of 4 Para take to the sea in commandeered fishing boats to make their way to Athens.

The 2nd Independent Parachute Brigade Group did not spend long in France. By 22 August it was back in Italy, and told to prepare to move to Greece, where the Germans were about to pull out because the Russian armies were working their way through the Balkans. The Western Allies decided to intervene to make sure that Communists did not get control of the country.

On 12 October C Company of 4th Para, with some engineers and a radio team, dropped on to the airfield at Megara, about 65 km (40 miles) west of Athens. The Germans were already pulling out of the Greek capital. The rest of the brigade arrived two days later, delayed by high winds. The Germans had blown up the road from Megara to Athens, so the Paras commandeered fishing boats and sailed along the coast, arriving in Athens to an enthusiastic welcome.

From then until February the brigade was employed in harassing the retreating Germans, and in intervening in a bitter civil war that had broken out among rival Greek factions. Its allies were the Greek royalists, and the principal opponents guerrillas belonging to ELAS, the National Popular Liberation Army. This was a Communist group, bent on capturing Athens. ELAS threw 25,000 soldiers into the battle for Athens, and lost about 4,000 killed or wounded, and 8,000 prisoners. It was a vicious campaign, and the various Greek factions did not hesitate to torture and murder each other. The brigade returned in February 1945 to Italy, where it stayed, inactive, until the Italian campaign ended. It was sent to Palestine in October 1945, when the war was nominally over.

EAST OF NOWHERE

The Paras chased the Germans up to the Albanian border. Near that frontier Lieutenant Nigel Riley led a platoon of B Company to sabotage the railway. The Paras cut the line, derailed a German troop train, and took 400 prisoners. Riley radioed a coded message announcing his success to his company commander, with a grid reference to show where he was. The code apparently distorted the message. He was asked to repeat it. Back came the reply:

START SWIMMING. YOUR POSITION PLACES YOU MIDDLE AEGEAN SEA. CONGRATULATIONS ON BLOWING UP ENEMY SUBMARINE. RETURN IMMEDIATELY TO BASE.

THE BATTLE OF NORMANDY, 1944

German armies invaded Russia on 22 June 1941, breaking a treaty which the two dictators, Adolf Hitler of Germany and Joseph Stalin of the Soviet Union, made in August 1939. By the end of October 1941 the Germans had driven through the Baltic states, Belarus and Ukraine, and were hammering at the gates of Moscow.

All through 1942 and 1943 Stalin called on his new allies, the British and Americans, to start a second front in the west, and so relieve the enormous pressure on the beleaguered Soviet forces. In Britain posters and graffiti proclaimed 'Second Front Now'. But in those years an operation of this magnitude was not possible, until a sufficient force had been built up in Britain to strike a decisive blow.

The North African campaign and the invasion of Sicily were a first step towards a second front. But everyone knew that Germany could only be defeated by an attack through France. And that meant a huge amphibious landing, the largest ever undertaken in any war. The Germans had created the Western Wall, a range of defences all along the Atlantic and English Channel coasts which would be very hard to break through.

Planning began in the summer of 1943, with a target date of sometime in May 1944, the earliest that sufficient forces could be ready. The target date became known as D-Day, and the starting time as H-Hour. Eisenhower was given the task of supreme commander, and the initial blow was to be commanded by

Below: Paras of Headquarters and Defence platoon, 5th Airborne Division, synchronize their watches after a briefing for Operation Overlord on 5 June 1944.

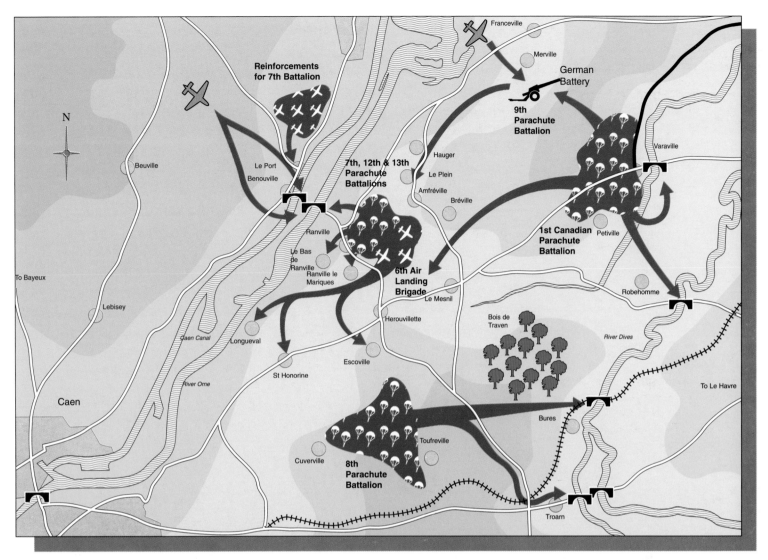

Map labels:
Franceville
Merville
German Battery
Reinforcements for 7th Battalion
9th Parachute Battalion
Varaville
N
Hauger
Le Plein
Amfréville
Bréville
7th, 12th & 13th Parachute Battalions
Beuville
Le Port Benouville
1st Canadian Parachute Battalion
Petiville
Ranville
Le Bas de Ranville
Ranville le Mariques
6th Air Landing Brigade
Le Mesnil
Robehomme
To Bayeux
Lebisey
Herouvillette
Bois de Traven
River Dives
Caen Canal
Longueval
Escoville
To Le Havre
River Orne
St Honorine
Bures
Caen
Toufreville
Cuverville
8th Parachute Battalion
Troarn

General Montgomery, who would for the first few weeks be commanding American as well as British troops. His American counterpart was to be General Omar Bradley, who would take over the US armies once the landing had been established. The whole campaign was given the code name 'Operation Overlord'.

PLANNING FOR D-DAY

The experience gained in North Africa and Sicily showed that airborne forces would be needed to start the operation, knocking on the door that infantry landing from the sea would have to force open. For the invasion a new Airborne Division, the 6th, was formed, and placed under the command of Major General

Richard Gale. The division included, besides the Paras, the Airlanding Brigade, which consisted of regular infantry who would be flown in by glider together with their weapons, artillery, and transport (Jeeps). The brigade was commanded by Brigadier the Honourable Hugh Kindersley. There were also a parachute squadron of Royal Engineers, a parachute field ambulance unit, and a host of other specialist units including signals and intelligence. All these units had to be welded into one body of troops who would work together in the coming invasion of Normandy. Gale began a programme of training immediately, while he was still awaiting the full complement of men he was to command.

Above: This is how 6th Airborne landed in Normandy on D-Day. 7, 12 and 13 Para were dropped east of the River Orne, about 6 kilometres (4 miles) north-west of Caen. The 6th Airlanding Brigade and its gliders landed in the same area. The Merville Battery is shown top right (see the detailed map on page 48).

There were two parachute brigades. The 3rd was commanded by Brigadier James Hill, fresh from his North African exploits. It included three battalions: 8 Para, commanded by Lieutenant Colonel Alastair Pearson, another veteran of North Africa; the newly formed 9 Para, commanded (except for the first few weeks) by Lieutenant Colonel Terence Otway; and the 1st (and only) Canadian Parachute Battalion, under the command of Lieutenant Colonel George Bradbrooke.

The 5th Parachute Brigade comprised 7 Para, led by Lieutenant Colonel Geoffrey Pine-Coffin ('Wooden Box' to his men); 12 Para, commanded (again after the first few weeks) by Lieutenant Colonel Johnny Johnson; and 13 Para, under Lieutenant Colonel Peter Luard. Each of the parachute battalions had a complement of 550 officers and other ranks, including a machine-gun platoon, a platoon with six 3-inch mortars, and three rifle companies.

The pilots who were to fly the gliders were organized into two regiments. They were volunteers from the Army and the Royal Air Force. Their gliders were the Horsas, which could carry up to 30 soldiers, and the Hamilcars, which could transport heavy guns and light tanks. Every pilot was expected to be able to fight

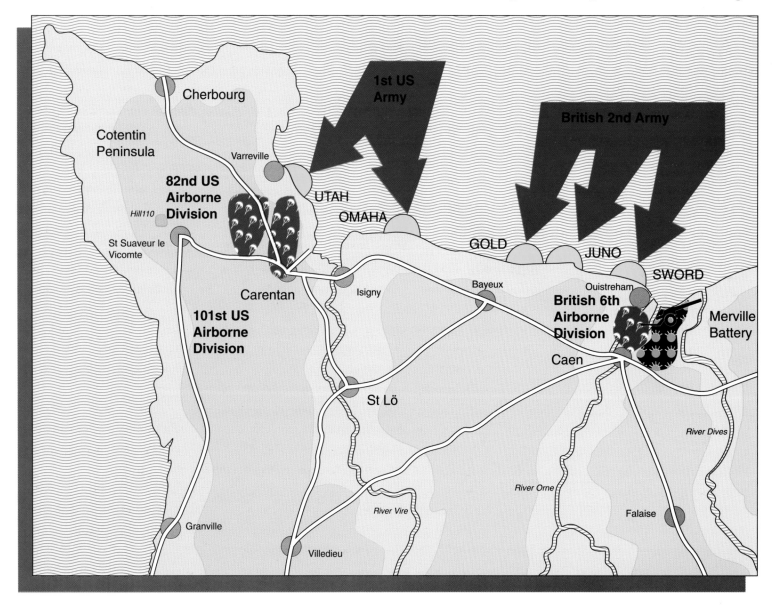

Above: A Horsa crash-landed in a cornfield during Overlord. The airborne troops in it are deploying behind a wall in readiness to advance. The slogan painted on the side of the glider reads 'Churchill's Reply'.

Left: The airborne attack on Normandy was timed for the period midnight to dawn on D-Day. US airborne troops landed in the Cotentin peninsula to soften up the German defences behind Utah beach, where the US seaborne troops landed at first light. The British 6th Airborne Division landed in a DZ just to the east of Sword beach, where ground troops of the 3rd British Division were due to land at dawn.

in the field once he had landed, though in practice they were mostly ferried back to England ready for more glider flights.

The 6th and 1st Airborne Divisions were under the overall command of Lieutenant General 'Boy' Browning; 1st Airborne were to be in action later, in the ill-fated Arnhem campaign.

ASSAULT FROM THE SKY

The sea landings were made on five beaches along the coast of Normandy. They were given the code names (from west to east) Utah, Omaha, Gold, Juno, and Sword. American troops landed on Utah and Omaha, and the British and Canadians on the other three.

Gale's orders were simple: between midnight and dawn of D-Day he was to land behind the German coastal defences to the east of Sword beach, capture the bridges on the main road over the River Orne and a canal linking the town of Caen with the sea; destroy a coastal battery near the mouth of the Orne which commanded Sword beach; and

in order to foil any counter-attack, destroy five bridges over the River Dives, which flowed east of the Orne; and capture and hold the high ground between the two rivers. He was to be reinforced about midday on D-Day by Commandos who were to land on Sword beach and fight their way inland.

Gale learned that the German 21st Panzer Division was in the area, and that the designated landing zones for his gliders were studded with posts and other obstacles. He decided on a bold stroke, and although it had to be modified at the last minute, this is how it worked out. At about 23.00 on the evening of 5 June, the eve of D-Day, six aircraft took off from Britain, carrying 60 Pathfinders from the 22nd Independent Parachute Company, whose job would be to locate Dropping Zones N and V.

Meanwhile 200 men in gliders, led by Major John Howard, had set off for a 'coup de main', their task being to crash-land at the two bridges which were to be captured and held until reinforcements arrived. Howard's men seized and held the bridges, and had fought off one counter-attack by the time the next wave of the assault came in.

DUCKS, BAKELITE

Brigadier Nigel Poett, the commander of 5th Parachute Brigade, dropped with the Pathfinders ahead of his brigade, so that he would be ready to take control if anything went wrong. His men were not far behind him. There was considerable confusion on the DZ, with men of various units muddled up. They had two methods of linking up. One was the challenge 'V' to which the response was 'for Victory'. This was a phrase much used in the dark days of World War II. The other was to rally to bird calls carried by officers, whose official designation was 'Ducks, bakelite, 1944 pattern'. The rallying call of 13 Para battalion was a hunting horn.

7 Para were widely scattered, and by 02.30 Lieutenant Colonel Pine-Coffin had collected only 200 men, but he led them to reinforce Major Howard at the bridges. 12 and 13 Para were also scattered, but were able to gather a sufficient force to complete their tasks. 13 Para had to clear a landing zone for the main airborne assault, removing poles and other obstacles. The main glider party arrived at about 03.30, 49 of the 72 gliders landing in a cornfield, their correct LZ. Of the other gliders, three made forced landings in England, three landed in the sea, and 14 were lost. One of the 14 was hit by anti-aircraft fire, but managed to crash-land in an orchard on the wrong side of the River Dives. The seven men aboard set out to walk to their rendezvous, aided by French

sympathizers who gave them directions. It took them five days and they covered 7 km (4 miles). On the way they ran into a German patrol of a car and two trucks, which they eliminated with hand grenades.

Gale came with the main glider force. Although the gliders were mostly wrecked, their passengers were unhurt and the equipment –

Men of a Royal Artillery battery watch 5 Para rallying to the call of 'Ducks, Bakelite, 1944 pattern' during Operation Mallard in June 1944.

RICHARD GALE

Richard Nelson Gale was a tall, spare man, with a ruddy complexion, bushy eyebrows and a 'Poona colonel' moustache. He had fought in several major battles in World War I, where he was awarded the MC, and subsequently served in India.

When World War II began he was a staff officer in the War Office, but was soon appointed to command the 5th Leicesters. In 1941 he was appointed to command the 1st Airborne Division, and then returned to the War Office as director of Airborne Forces. At the time he was given 6th Airborne Division he was 47 years old.

In spite of his conventional appearance, Gale was a born leader, able to devise plans, carry them out, and inspire his men. He was in short the ideal man to lead the assault on the West Wall.

He also had the right troops to lead. At the end of D-Day plus 1 he wrote: 'I thanked God for the courage of the troops: they were splendid. Quiet in their strength and great in their skill, they lived up to the traditions of the British Army. The light of God was in their eyes.'

guns and jeeps – survived. They set out in column towards their rendezvous, the church at the village of Ranville. When the column ground to a halt, a booming voice was heard saying: 'Don't you dare to argue with me, Richard Gale. Get on, I say, get on.' They got on.

BLOWING BRIDGES

The parachute battalions charged with blowing the bridges over the River Dives were dropped over a wide area, some landing in marshes, others in trees. 8 Para (the Canadians) had as their target the bridges at Robehomme and Varaville. Lieutenant Norman Toseland managed to collect enough men, some from other battalions, to make their way to the Robehomme bridge. A French girl guided them. They reached the bridge soon after 03.00 hours, but had only enough explosives to weaken it. Fortunately, another party with more explosives arrived about three hours later and the bridge was destroyed.

Major Murray McLeod, commander of C Company, was supposed to attack the Varaville Bridge with 100 men. In the event he had to set out with 15. He took up a position in the village overlooking the bridge. They held it for some time, with heavy loss (including McLeod himself), until they heard a massive explosion: another group under a sergeant had reached the bridge and destroyed it. Later the German garrison at Varaville surrendered.

The bridges at Bures were destroyed by 8 Para led by Lieutenant Colonel Pearson. The

The bridge over the Orne, later renamed Pegasus Bridge, the objective of Howard's 'coup de main' party on 6 June 1944 and the first area of France to be recaptured by the Allies on D-Day.

bridge at Troarn was still intact by 09.15, but Major Tim Roseveare and seven sappers, who had landed by glider some distance from their LZ, set out in a jeep, forced their way through the town with machine-guns blazing, blew a hole in the bridge and escaped on foot. Another party later fought their way into Troarn, and increased the gap in the bridge to 20 m (70 ft).

MERVILLE BATTERY

The destruction of Merville Battery, overlooking Sword beach, was assigned to 9 Para. A reconnaissance party landed safely on the DZ, but the lights they put out to guide the

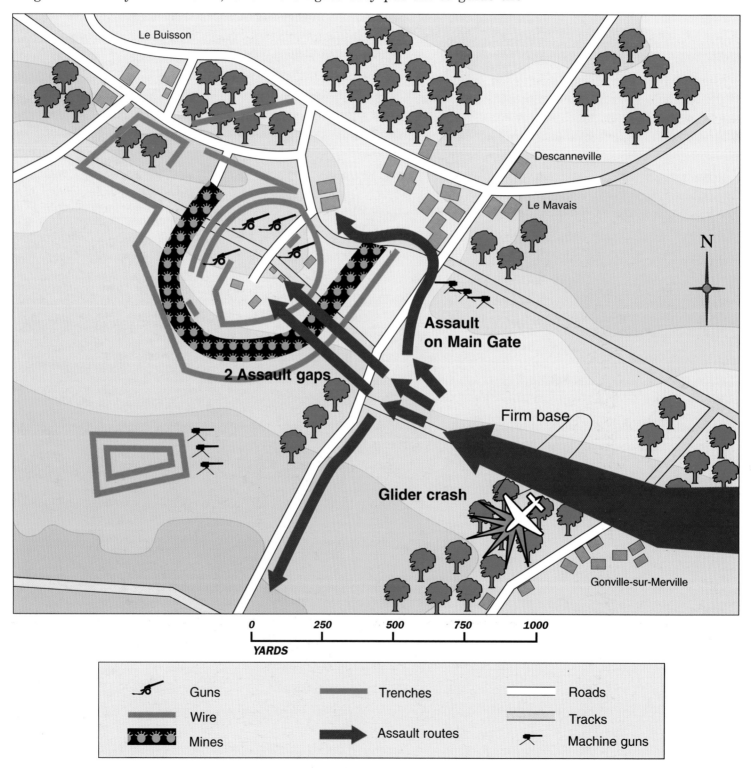

Le Buisson

Descanneville

Le Mavais

N

**Assault
on Main Gate**

2 Assault gaps

Firm base

Glider crash

Gonville-sur-Merville

0   250   500   750   1000

YARDS

Guns	Trenches	Roads
Wire		Tracks
Mines	Assault routes	Machine guns

main party were obscured by smoke from a bombing raid, and by 02.30 Lieutenant Colonel Otway could gather only 150 of his 550-strong battalion. Gliders which were supposed to bring in an assault party with jeeps and anti-tank guns had not arrived. With only three hours left before the battery was supposed to be destroyed, Otway decided to attack with what force he had.

The advance party had already cut their way through the perimeter fence of the battery, and marked out a path through the minefield inside. Otway and his men rushed forward, firing Bren guns and hurling grenades. After a brisk fight they overcame the German garrison, and tried to put the guns out of action without explosives. They lost 80 killed and wounded out of their 150. Meanwhile, two gliders had reached Merville. One landed 3 km (2 miles) away, but the other came to rest in a nearby orchard, and was able to re-inforce Otway. The guns remained intact until the Germans evacuated the battery some time later.

HOLDING ON

At the end of the second day 6th Airborne Division were holding a defensive line on the east bank of the River Dives. They had gained all their objectives except for a small strip of the coast, but they were well under strength, with 800 killed and wounded and more than a thousand men still trying to find their way from their drop zones.

The Germans made a series of counter-attacks, and on July 10 they launched a ferocious attack on the village of Bréville, which was in the Paras' defensive line. The enemy opened up a gap, which the Paras

tried to close, with heavy losses. Gale decided to make a final counter-attack, suspecting that no matter how exhausted his men were, the Germans were probably more so. His reserve was 12 Para, reduced to 300 men but refreshed by several hours' rest, a company of the Devonshire Regiment, and some tanks and artillery. Lieutenant Colonel Johnston, 12 Para's commander, was killed, but Colonel Reggie Parker, deputy commander of the 6th Airlanding Brigade, took over and within an hour the village was retaken and the gap in the line was closed.

The Airborne Division held that line for about 10 weeks, until a general advance supported by Dutch and Belgian regiments was ordered. They swept forward until they reached the outskirts of Le Havre. They covered 70 km (45 miles), captured a thousand prisoners and harried the enemy ceaselessly. At the end of September the Division was withdrawn to England for a much-needed rest. It had suffered 821 killed, 2,709 wounded, and 927 missing.

Left: The attack on Merville Battery. Lt. Col. Otway of 9 Para gathered his 150-strong force near Gonville-sur-Merville. It had one medium machine-gun. An advance party cut its way through the perimeter fence around the battery and staked out a route through the minefield. Otway and his party then rushed the garrison, which they overcame, but without explosives they were unable to put the guns out of action completely.

Below: The success of the Airborne landings was due to the bold strategy of Major General Richard Gale, who had a glider force crash-land at two of the river bridges in the east, surprising the Germans. This Horsa crash-landed near the Troarn Bridge, which British Army sappers succeeded in putting out of action completely after two attempts.

THE TRAGEDY OF ARNHEM, 1944

Below: The map clearly shows what went wrong at Arnhem. The main DZs were 13 kilometres (8 miles) from the target bridges, leaving the Paras a long drive to reach their objective. If a daring blow had been struck and some Paras had landed close to the road-bridge, they would have captured it without difficulty – it was undefended. The supply dropping point (V) was unavailable because of a heavy German presence. In any case bad weather made supply difficult.

The Arnhem campaign in World War II was like the Dardanelles campaign in World War I: a bold stroke designed to shorten the war. And like the Dardanelles episode it went disastrously wrong.

After the Battle of Normandy the German armies were on the run. They were retreating as fast as they had advanced in the Blitzkrieg of 1940. By the middle of September the British 2nd Army had driven through France and Belgium, and was engaged in the Netherlands. The way into Germany was barred by waterways: the River Maas (called the Meuse upstream in France); the River Waal, which is the southern and main branch of the mighty River Rhine; and the Lower Rhine to the north of the Waal. East of the Maas, which flows north when it enters the Netherlands, was the German frontier, guarded by the Siegfried Line, a mighty defence line which stopped in the north at the Rhine.

At the time the Germans were launching V2 rocket bombs against Britain from sites along the Dutch coast. These huge rockets arrived without warning at their targets: the first you knew was the bang, and the destruction and civilian casualties each caused were considerable. It was highly desirable to put the V2s out of action.

There was some conflict in the Allied high command as to what to

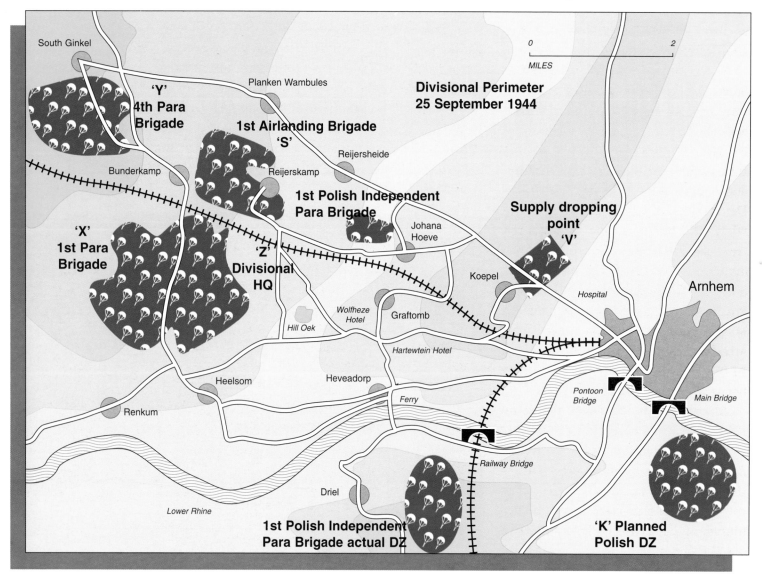

do next. Eisenhower wanted to advance on a broad front, and he was anxious to support the 12th US Army Group under General Omar Bradley, which was making good progress in the east, and especially the 3rd US Army in that group whose commander, the dashing George E. Patton, was making spectacular advances. Montgomery wanted to strike north, capture the bridges over the river barriers and clear the English Channel coast, thus putting the V2 rockets out of action. He also thought that such a move would shorten the war, and enable Germany to be defeated before Christmas 1944. After considerable argument Eisenhower agreed that an airborne attack should be made on the bridges over the three main rivers and five smaller waterways.

So Operation Market Garden was born. 'Market' was the codename for the airborne strike, while 'Garden' was the follow-up and reinforcement by the armoured columns of the British 2nd Army under its commander, Lieutenant General Sir Miles Dempsey. The task was to drive an 80-km (50-mile) corridor through the German defences. Three airborne divisions were involved, one British and two American. It was to be the greatest air strike of the war, much bigger than the airborne part of the attack on Normandy, which involved 17,000 men, parachutists, and glider-borne forces.

Although this is a book about the Paras, it is impossible to consider their operations, especially at Arnhem, without covering the rest of the Airborne forces, of which they were a part. In the words of the popular song, you couldn't have one without the other.

MONTY
1887–1976

Bernard Law Montgomery was one of the greatest generals of World War II; he inspired the men he led, and got on well with them; but his manner and methods of command made him disliked by the American generals he had to work with. Monty, as he was often called, was born in 1887, the son of a London vicar. He joined the army in 1907, and went through World War I, starting as a lieutenant and ending as chief of staff of a division. Having seen the muddle and lack of communication between the staff and the men in the field, Montgomery decided to learn his job properly.

When World War II began in 1939 he was a major general, and went to France with the British Expeditionary Force (BEF). In the dark days of 1940 he was one of the two generals who supervised the evacuation of British soldiers from the beaches at Dunkirk. In August 1942 he was appointed to command the 8th Army in Egypt, where he planned and won the decisive Battle of El Alamein.

There he evolved the way of life and command which was to become his trademark. He had a caravan as a tactical HQ; he neither smoked nor drank, and was never 'one of the boys'; a widower, he shunned the company of women. Having made a decision, he refused to be bogged down in details. He communicated with his subordinate commanders – and often with his superiors – through his chief of staff, Francis de Guingand; this was resented, but Montgomery knew that de Guingand was more tactful than he and could put a point better than he could. Montgomery always wore battledress instead of a more formal uniform. His headgear was a black beret with two badges in it. The two badges started as a joke but became an instantly recognizable trademark. Montgomery was, in the words of his chief, Eisenhower, 'a master in the methodical preparation of forces for a set-piece attack'.

This was why he was chosen to lead the assault on Normandy. After the war Montgomery, then a field marshal, commanded the British forces occupying Germany. He was subsequently Chief of the Imperial General Staff, the head of the whole British army, 1946–48, and deputy supreme commander, under Eisenhower, of the North Atlantic Treaty Organization forces in Europe, 1951–58. But he remained controversial to the last.

THE ATTACK BEGINS

The force chosen for Operation Market Garden was the 1st Airborne Corps, commanded by Lieutenant General 'Boy' Browning, which consisted of the 1st British and the 82nd and 101st US Airborne Divisions. The two American parachute divisions were given three giant bridges to capture, those over the River Maas at Grave, the River Waal at Nijmegen, and the Maas-Waal canal. The British division was to go further north and capture the road-bridge over the River Rhine at Arnhem, the 'bridge too far' of later legend.

The big problem was transport: 2,495 aircraft were needed to carry parachutists, and 1,295 to tow gliders. But only 1,545 planes were available. This meant that the troops would have to be landed in three waves.

The British 1st Airborne Division was commanded by Major General Robert Urquhart, a veteran of 8th Army and the Sicily landings. It contained the 1st and 4th Parachute Brigades, commanded respectively by Brigadier Gerald Lathbury, who had recovered from the wounds he sustained in Sicily, and Brigadier John Hackett, a veteran of the Western Desert campaigns. The third brigade in the division was 1st Airlanding Brigade, commanded by Brigadier Philip Hicks, the man who had to swim to shore when his glider landed in the sea off Sicily. Urquhart decided to drop his parachutists in a clear area some 13 km (8 miles) west of the two Arnhem bridges, and north

Below: Arnhem bridge, the objective of 2 Para during Operation Garden, and the 'bridge too far' of later legend.

Above: A knocked-out 6-pounder anti-tank gun of the 1st Airlanding Anti-Tank Battery, evidence of the tough fight 2 Para faced during their advance towards Oosterbeek during the Arnhem campaign.

of the Rhine. The disadvantage of this decision was that to secure a safe DZ he was sacrificing the element of surprise, and relying on continued fine weather to send in the second wave.

As soon as the corridor was cleared, a land force of two infantry divisions and the Guards Armoured Division (a tank force) was to move up as reinforcements. This force was under the command of Lieutenant General Brian Horrocks.

THE LUCK OF THE GERMANS

While the weather was the main worry for the British commanders, they had an unknown quantity to deal with: the Germans. Were they prepared for such a bold attack? They were in fact taken by surprise when the Allied planes roared over the Netherlands, preceded by more than 1,000 bombers which tried to neutralize the anti-aircraft batteries along the coast, and protected by 1,240 fighter planes.

But as it happened the first landings were witnessed by the commander of the 1st German Parachute Army, General Kurt Student, who had led the parachute invasion of

Crete. He was holding a line south of Arnhem along one of the Maas canals. As the planes roared overhead he exclaimed: 'Oh, how I wish that I had ever had such a powerful force at my disposal!'

Also on the spot was Field Marshal Walter Model, commanding Army Group B. He was one of Hitler's most successful and resourceful generals. He had his headquarters at Oosterbeek, close to Arnhem. As he saw the British parachutists descending he drove into the town and took command of its defence. So the two generals whose job it was to defend the Netherlands were so placed that they could act quickly to repel the attack. In the wreck of a glider that had been shot down the Germans found a copy of the orders for the whole operation, and the two commanders knew exactly how to deploy their slender reserves.

THE LANDING

For months the men of 1st Airborne had been waiting impatiently in England while their comrades of 6th Airborne were fighting the Battle of Normandy. A dozen times or more they had prepared to take off on an operation, only to have it cancelled at the last minute. They were trained to the nth degree, and were burning to get into action before the war was over. Some of them had started to refer to themselves as 'The Stillborn Division'. Many of Lathbury's 1st Parachute Brigade had been in action in Sicily. Hackett's men of the 4th Brigade had never been in battle, yet they were all eager.

The American Army Air Force, which was supplying a large part of the troop carriers and towing planes, was not used to night operations. Its

pilots insisted on flying by day when they could see where they were and find the DZs easily. They ignored the fact that however weak the German air force was by this point in the war, the anti-aircraft batteries were strong. Many of the German planes were grounded by lack of fuel. The planners organizing the air drops insisted on the Paras landing a safe distance away from their objectives and the guns that protected them.

On Sunday 17 September, the parachutes and gliders of 1st Airborne landed safely on their DZ and LZ 13 km (8 miles) west of Arnhem. Only about 38 gliders failed to arrive, because their tow-ropes broke, but they had most of the armoured jeeps which were to be used to rush the two bridges, rail and road, in Arnhem. Despite this 2 Para under Lieutenant Colonel Frost set off briskly towards the bridges. Just as they reached the rail bridge near the suburb of Oosterbeek the Germans blew it up. The road bridge was unguarded until dusk when a company of German SS troops drove up and secured the southern end. Soon after Frost's men seized the northern end. An attempt to cross the bridge was thwarted by heavy German fire. At this point one of Frost's officers commented bitterly: 'As far as I can tell we've jumped into a grand military cock-up.' A sergeant put it even more bluntly: 'As you might expect , sir – the biggest f-up since Mons.' Mons was the first battle of World War I, and ended in a British retreat.

Below: One of the two medieval churches in Arnhem, this one situated just north of the bridge. The fierce fighting extended beyond the bridge and into the town where 1, 3 and 11 Para suffered many casualties

HEAVY FIGHTING

Near their DZ, 1 and 3 Para were trying to advance on a more direct route to Arnhem than the riverbank road used by 2 Para. They were held up by heavy opposition, at first by a training battalion, and soon by part of 9th SS, with tanks and armoured cars. Fighting was fierce, and the Paras suffered many casualties. Next day 1 Para, now down to 100 men, switched to the route taken by 2 Para, but by then the Germans were in place in strength. Two companies of the South Staffordshire Regiment went to help them, but they could make little progress. Urquhart, the divisional commander, was cut off in Arnhem, hiding in a house with a German self-propelled gun outside, cutting off his escape.

At the bridge Frost waited with 500 men and one anti-tank gun for the back-up that never came. Hick and the Airlanding Brigade were under orders to wait for reinforcements from England, due at 10.00 hours the next day. So they did. The result was stalemate, giving the Germans ample time to prepare their defensive moves.

Back at the bridge, Frost's men were holed up in some houses. The Germans began attacking at dawn, and the attacks went on all day. By 15.30 hours Frost was short of food, and was fast running out of ammunition. He had been asked to take command of the 1st Brigade, Lathbury having vanished (he was hiding in a friendly Dutch house, wounded and unable to walk).

REINFORCEMENTS

The 4th Parachute Brigade began dropping at 15.00 hours on the Monday, five hours late because of fog in England. Their commander, Hackett, found Hick in temporary command of the division in Urquhart's absence. Hackett at once took over from Hick and decided to try to reach Arnhem by a more northerly route, north of the railway line. He did not realize that a perfectly good ferry was working across the river at Heveadorp, about 6 km (4 miles) from Arnhem. This would have enabled a strong force to move to the southern end of the bridge. At about 19.00 hours Urquhart rejoined his headquarters, the German gun having moved away.

LONSDALE FORCE

In the town 1 Para, 3 Para, 11 Para, and the South Staffords had been cut to pieces, and many of 11 Para had been forced to surrender. The rest made their way back to a line near Oosterbeek Church, where Major Dickie Lonsdale, second in command of 11 Para, took charge. There were only about 250 men left. Lonsdale mustered them in the church and from the pulpit told them that they must fight for their lives, dig in, and make every shot tell as they were short of ammunition. He gave them the name of Lonsdale Force.

By the evening of Tuesday, Frost had only 140 men left. The Germans were attacking from the north, and the houses the Paras were holding were either collapsing or on fire. Frost himself was wounded and Major Freddy Gough took over. In the cellars of the burning buildings were 200 wounded

Below: Life goes on – BBC reporter Stanley Maxstead writes his report of the battle from a position of relative safety.

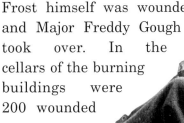

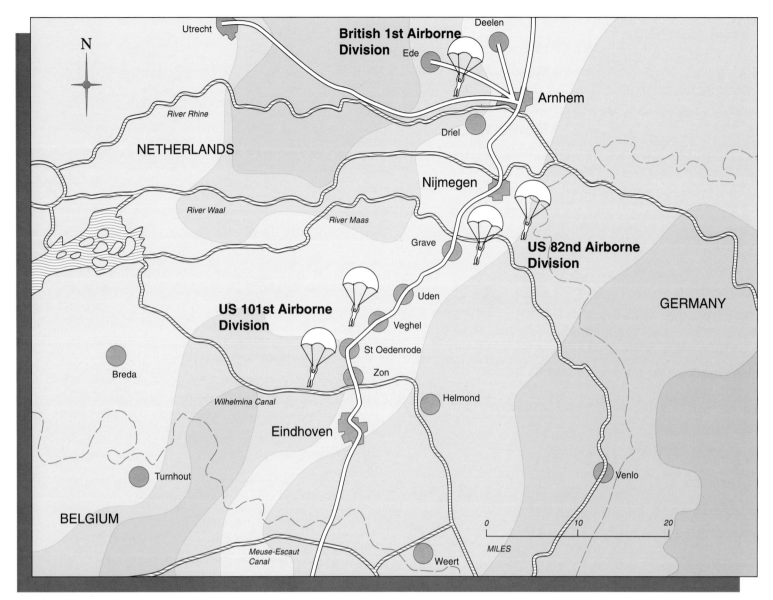

Above: Operation Market Garden, September 1944. Market Garden was a two-part operation: Market was the seizure of briges by Paras; Garden was the advance of the main troops once the bridges were secured. There were three main barriers, the rivers Rhine, Waal, and Maas, plus five minor ones, including the Wilhelmina Canal, shown here. All were captured except the two most important ones: the road and rail bridges over the Rhine at Arnhem.

men. The Paras arranged a mercy truce with the Germans, who carried the wounded out to safety. Fighting then resumed, but not for long. At 09.00 hours on Thursday morning the Paras were overrun and the survivors, many wounded, dispersed or were taken prisoner.

The rest of the Paras fighting in the outskirts of Arnhem battled on until the night of 25/26 September, when evacuation was ordered. Many, including the wounded, were captured; others were hidden and helped by friendly Dutch civilians. Lathbury, who had been taken to hospital, was able to move after a day or two, and crept out in the middle of the night,

escaping into woods, where he hid for most of a week. Eventually the Germans began evacuating the civilian population of the area. In the confusion Lathbury and about 80 other stragglers assembled and calmly walked past Germans to freedom.

The final casualty list was high. Of the 10,000 men who landed north of the Rhine 1,130 were killed, and 6,450 were taken prisoner, half of them wounded. Only about 2,200 reached safety.

The rest of Operation Market Garden was a success. Seven bridges were captured, and the corridor along which Horrocks's three divisions had advanced was firmly held.

WHAT WENT WRONG?

There were several main reasons for the failure of the Arnhem operation. Montgomery himself identified four, and others have amplified his list.

The first was that Supreme Headquarters did not regard the operation as the spearhead of a major Allied move to isolate and eventually to occupy the Ruhr, the heartland of Germany's industrial power. Thus, Eisenhower's orders, which in essence were to give priority to this knock-out punch and scale down operations elsewhere on the front, were not fully carried out.

The second, and probably biggest, error was in dropping the airborne forces too far from the Arnhem bridges. Had a complete parachute brigade been dropped close to the bridges the road-bridge at least could have been captured easily, within a matter of minutes. Montgomery blamed himself for not ordering this to be done. Part of the trouble in this respect was that Urquhart was reluctant to incur heavy casualties in a 'coup de main' such as was carried out by Gale in Normandy. In the event, he lost many more men in the bloody fighting in Arnhem than he would have done in a daring stroke. In hindsight he realized this.

The third problem was the weather, which turned against the invading forces, hampering the drops and slowing down the bringing in of re-inforcements.

And the fourth was the presence of the 22nd German Panzer Corps, which was refitting in the Arnhem area and was therefore on the spot to repel the attack. The Allies knew the Corps was there, but thought that after the mauling it had received in Normandy it would not be able to fight effectively. The lesson here was that in war one should never under-estimate one's opponent.

Another factor, not listed by Montgomery, was that the radio com-munications did not always work properly. Poor communications have been the cause of much trouble in the world, and especially in war. The British and Americans should have known this and made every effort to improve communications.

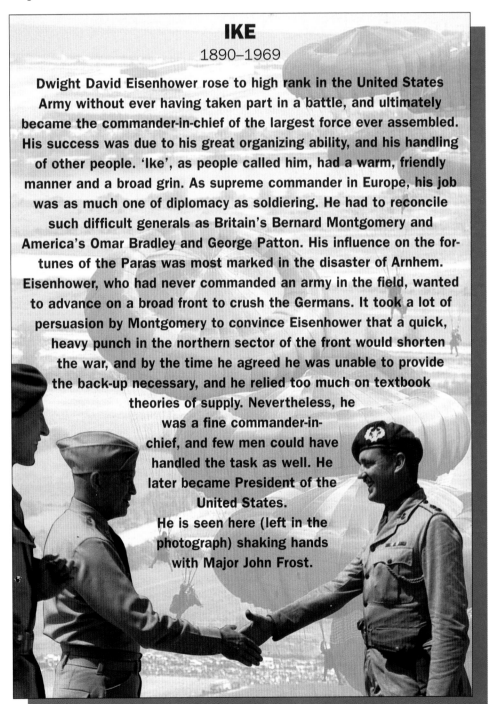

IKE
1890–1969

Dwight David Eisenhower rose to high rank in the United States Army without ever having taken part in a battle, and ultimately became the commander-in-chief of the largest force ever assembled. His success was due to his great organizing ability, and his handling of other people. 'Ike', as people called him, had a warm, friendly manner and a broad grin. As supreme commander in Europe, his job was as much one of diplomacy as soldiering. He had to reconcile such difficult generals as Britain's Bernard Montgomery and America's Omar Bradley and George Patton. His influence on the for-tunes of the Paras was most marked in the disaster of Arnhem. Eisenhower, who had never commanded an army in the field, wanted to advance on a broad front to crush the Germans. It took a lot of persuasion by Montgomery to convince Eisenhower that a quick, heavy punch in the northern sector of the front would shorten the war, and by the time he agreed he was unable to provide the back-up necessary, and he relied too much on textbook theories of supply. Nevertheless, he was a fine commander-in-chief, and few men could have handled the task as well. He later became President of the United States. He is seen here (left in the photograph) shaking hands with Major John Frost.

THE BATTLE OF THE BULGE, 1945

Below: A devastating foe – the German King Tiger tank, which only the heaviest of the Russian tanks could match. Around Bure the Shermans brought up to support 13 Para were devastated by the Tigers' firepower.

Having extended his forces along a 960-km (600-mile) front, Eisenhower suddenly found himself with a logistical problem: he could not send to all his forces sufficient supplies to do more than hold the line. Although the Arnhem campaign had opened the way to clearing the French, Belgian, and Dutch ports – particularly Antwerp – this task took longer than either he or Montgomery had bargained for.

Thousands of troops were waiting in the US to be shipped with their weapons and other supplies direct to continental Europe. Their equipment was packed in large crates, and even

when the Channel ports reopened, so much damage had been done that they were working well below capacity. For example, they lacked the cranes needed to unload the large crates, which had to be unloaded in England, repacked in smaller quantities and ferried across.

This gave Hitler a badly needed breathing space, because the German armies in the west were in a much worse state than the Allied armies. Much of their equipment had been lost or destroyed, and thousands of men were taken prisoner. Hitler and General Alfred Jodl, his chief of staff, planned a bold stroke

Above: The bridge at the German-held village of Bure, the objective of 13 Para Battalion during the battle of the Bulge, January 1945.

which would enable them to recapture Antwerp, cut off the Allied armies to the north of that port, and force the Allies to consider a compromise peace.

The attack was to be launched through the Ardennes, a region of mountains and forest extending from northern France into Belgium and Luxembourg. It is traversed by rapid rivers flowing in deep valleys, and includes areas of bog and moorland. Trees cover about half the area. The area was fought over during World War I, and so the Germans were familiar with the terrain.

The offensive was Hitler's plan, and not all his generals thought it would work. But he had managed to build up a stronger force than they had believed possible, and he was full of confidence. In the early hours of 16 December Hitler struck, choosing a section of the front which was only thinly held by the American armies. Incidentally the attack brought the British 6th Airborne Division back into action.

THE BULGE IS FORMED

Hitler's attack was in force. A creeping barrage by 2,000 guns, plus salvoes of V1 rocket planes, the 'flying bombs' or 'doodlebugs' all too familiar to British civilians, preceded an advance by 14 infantry divisions supported by five panzer (armoured) divisions. Parties of parachutists and saboteurs dressed in civilian or American army uniforms added to the confusion. Within seven days the Germans had punched a hole through the American troops holding this rather thinly defended part of the line, and created a salient 70 km (45 miles) deep. The shape of this salient gave rise to what became called the Battle of the Bulge. The Germans aimed to drive a wedge between the British forces in the north and the Americans in the south, and prevent an Allied attack on Germany itself.

The Americans, including the high command, were taken completely by surprise, and their reactions were accordingly somewhat slow. Within days Bradley's command had been split, and he lost contact with his armies north of the Bulge. Eisenhower realized that the only thing to do was to put the northern part of Bradley's forces under the command of one man. That man had to be Montgomery, who was in place and had the organization and the forces to take over. He had in fact already begun deploying some of his own troops to head off an advance into the region between the River Meuse (Maas) and Brussels.

Putting Montgomery in command of American troops was greatly resented by Bradley and his staff, the ground troops, and by the American public back home. Montgomery's air of confidence, designed to inspire the troops, instead infuriated them. But Eisenhower had no alternative, and he was too big a man to allow other people's personal feelings to affect this military decision.

A CHRISTMAS TRIP

The 6th Airborne Division received a severe mauling in Normandy, and heavy casualties. For example, 1 Canadian Paras had lost 24 of their 27 officers, and 343 out of 516 other ranks. The division had also lost its commander, Major General Richard Gale, who had been promoted. But by the end of 1944 they had been re-equipped, their numbers had been made up by fresh volunteers, they had retrained, and they were ready for action. They were soon needed.

To help plug the Ardennes gap, Montgomery called on 6th Airborne, many of whose men were on Christmas leave or about to depart. Their new commander, Major General Eric Bols, received their orders on 20 December 1944, and the

division was ready to leave for Belgium on Christmas Eve, some by air, others by sea. By Boxing Day 6th Airborne was concentrated in an area between Dinant and Namur, relieving the US 84th Infantry Division. The weather was bitterly cold, with thick snow and temperatures of –22°C (–8°F). Night patrols wrapped themselves in white sheets as camouflage against the white snow.

By then the German advance had been halted, partly because of the stout American defence of the little town of Bastogne, which was surrounded. The Germans called on the

Above: A patrol of 13 Para, wearing white camouflage gear, advancing through the snow during the battle of the Bulge.

THE GERMAN SABOTEURS

One of the most daring parts of the German attack was led by a panzer commander, Otto Skorzeny. As planned, parties of German saboteurs riding in captured American tanks and wearing American uniforms were to slip ahead of the main force and create mayhem. About 40 jeep-loads of these men, all speaking American-English, got through, and some even reached the River Meuse. Their activities included cutting telephone wires, capturing dispatch riders, and damaging radio stations. They killed military policemen who were stationed to direct convoys of US military vehicles advancing to the front. One man even took over the work of a policeman, and managed to direct a US convoy down the wrong road.

garrison to surrender, to which its commander, Brigadier General A. C. McAuliffe, replied 'Nuts!' It was in these circumstances that 6th Airborne was ordered to attack the tip of the German salient, with 13 Para, part of the 3rd Parachute Brigade, attacking Bure, a strongly held village. A Company led the advance on Bure, wading through deep snow, while B Company tried to take the high ground to the right. They came under heavy fire: A Company lost a third of its men in a few minutes, and B Company was even harder hit. However, A Company entered the village and began clearing it house by house, still losing men. The Germans brought up Tiger tanks, with which they did enormous damage. Infantry which came up to support the Paras brought with them some Sherman tanks, but these were quickly knocked out by the more powerful Tigers. Eventually Bure was taken, and 13 Para withdrew, having lost seven officers and 182 other ranks, 68 of them killed.

Life in thick snow and sub-zero temperatures continued to be difficult. A patrol of 22nd Independent Parachute company accidentally strayed into a minefield. Several men trod on mines and were wounded. A medical officer ordered everyone to stay where they were. He walked into the minefield and carried out emergency first-aid. Two sergeants arrived with mine detectors and cleared a path through the minefield. When they rescued the medical officer and a casualty he was supporting, they found three mines close round them.

At the end of January, 6th Airborne was moved to the Netherlands, where they carried out patrols in flooded conditions for three weeks. The division was then withdrawn to England. The Battle of the Bulge was effectively over by 25 January, by which time the Germans had been pushed back to their original line. The battle cost the Germans 250,000 casualties, against 60,000 for the Allies, and all it did was to postpone the Allied advance into Germany for six weeks.

Below: British Churchill tanks moving to support 6th Airborne Division during the Battle of the Bulge. The Churchills were the main British tanks, but were no match for the German Tigers.

THE RHINE CROSSING, 1945

Once the Battle of the Bulge was over the Allies prepared for the decisive stroke: the crossing of the River Rhine and the invasion of Germany. There were still severe tensions between the Americans and the British, and a British proposal to bring Alexander over from Italy to become Eisenhower's deputy in place of Tedder, with the idea that he could relieve Eisenhower of some of his responsibilities for the land battle, raised a furious storm. The proposal was opposed not only by the Americans but very strongly by Montgomery, and was dropped.

Eisenhower's arrangements for the crossing of the Rhine involved leaving 9th US Army under Montgomery's command for the northern attack. This upset Bradley and Patton, who believed, wrongly, that it was Montgomery's idea. However, it was not the only transfer of command: the British 6th Airborne Division was combined with the 17th US Airborne Division to form 18th US Airborne Corps, under the command of the the American Major General Matthew Ridgeway. Major General Richard Gale was Ridgeway's second in command. The whole corps was part of Montgomery's overall command.

Montgomery had two armies: the British 2nd Army, under Lieutenant General Sir Miles Dempsey, and the US 9th Army under Lieutenant General W. H. Simpson. His orders from Eisenhower were to seize the west bank of the Rhine from Nijmegen to Düsseldorf. The plan he evolved to carry out Eisenhower's orders was for a crossing to be made north of the Ruhr, with 2nd Army on the left and 9th Army on the right. A bridgehead would also be established by the airborne forces. This was the last phase of the war, and once again

Below: 8th Para Battalion receive last-minute instructions before emplaning for the Rhine Crossing operation in March 1945.

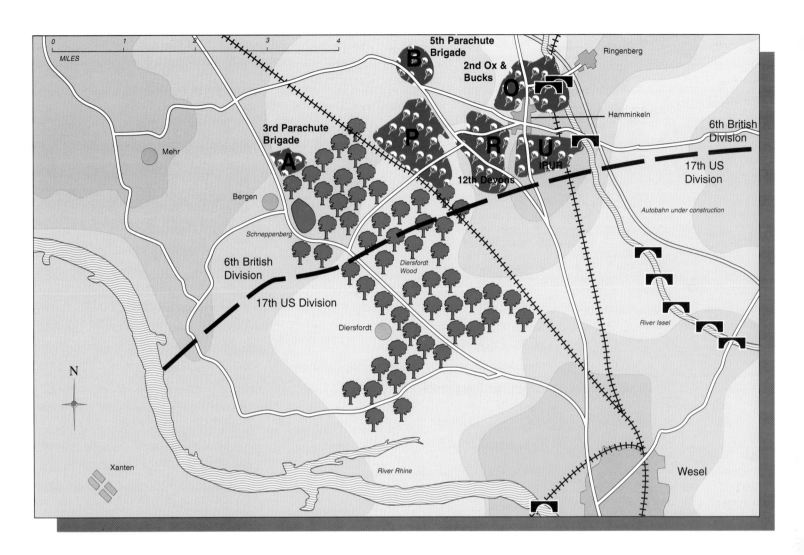

the Paras were to play an important part in the campaign.

OPERATION VERITABLE

The overall attack had the codename Veritable, the Rhine crossing was called Plunder, and the airborne part of that was called Varsity. Veritable began with a bang – a huge artillery barrage – on 8 February, along a line from Nijmegen to south of Strasbourg. Montgomery's first task was to advance to the west bank of the Rhine. The Canadian 1st Army and 30th British Corps began the northern attack, driving south from Nijmegen through the forested area of the Reichswald, reaching the Rhine on 13 February. Further south the Allied armies had to cross the River Roer, which was then in flood.

Meanwhile, 18th US Airborne Corps was hard at work preparing for Operation Varsity. Officers, NCOs, and other ranks were briefed on their objectives, LZs, and DZs with the aid of aerial photographs and models. The lessons of Normandy and Arnhem had been learned, and the Paras and gliders were to land as close as possible to their objectives. Artillery bombardment and heavy bombing were laid on, to continue until 40 minutes before the landing time. Major General Eric Bols was in command of 6th Airborne. Brigadier James Hill, commander of 3rd Parachute Brigade, gave a pep talk to his men, in the course of which he stressed that the enemy was likely to be thoroughly demoralized by the preliminary bombardment and the

Above: The plan for Operation Varsity. A and B are Dropping Zones (DZs), while O, P, R, and U are Landing Zones (LZs) for the glider-borne troops. LZ P was used by 2nd Airlanding Anti-Tank Regiment, Royal Artillery, who suffered heavy casualties during their landing.

Above: One of the 440 gliders involved in 6th Airborne Division's attack on German positions along the Rhine, codenamed Operation Varsity. The attack caught the enemy by surprise and during the first day of operations many German prisoners were taken.

Below: Unloading a quick-firing AA gun from a Horsa glider to go into action during the Rhine Crossing operation in March 1945.

sight of fierce paratroopers dropping from the sky, adding: 'You needn't think, just because you hear a few stray bullets flying about, that some miserable Hun is shooting at you. That is a form of egotism. But if by any chance you happen to meet one of these Huns in person, you will treat him, gentlemen, with extreme disfavour.' It was in that spirit the Paras set out on their last great campaign of the war.

OPERATION VARSITY

Operation Varsity began on 24 March. A fleet of 242 Dakota bombers and 440 gliders took off from England just before dawn, carrying 6th Airborne Division. A similar fleet flying alongside carried 17th US Airborne Division. The element of surprise was enhanced because Commandos and infantry had begun crossing the Rhine in assault craft the night before. The Germans would have expected the parachutists to be the spearhead of the attack.

The British 3rd Parachute Brigade dropped right on target, exactly as planned. 8 Para was the first battalion to land, followed by brigade headquarters, 1 Canadian

THE DIVISION'S VC

One man in 6th Airborne was awarded the Victoria Cross. He was Corporal George Topham, a medical orderly of 1 Canadian Para. A wounded man was lying out in the open. Two orderlies went to rescue him, but were shot and killed. Without hesitation Topham went to the wounded man, ignoring heavy fire, and carried out first aid. He himself was shot through the nose, but he ignored the wound and carried the man back to safety.

The official citation continued: 'During the next two hours Corporal Topham refused all offers of medical help for his own wound. He worked most devotedly throughout this period to bring wounded in, showing complete disregard for heavy and accurate enemy fire. It was only when all casualties had been cleared that he consented to his own wound being treated. His immediate evacuation was ordered but he interceded so earnestly on his own behalf that he was eventually allowed to return to duty.

'On his way back to his company he came across a carrier which had received a direct hit. Enemy mortar bombs were still dropping around, the carrier itself was burning fiercely and its own mortar ammunition was exploding. An experienced officer on the spot had warned all not to approach the carrier.

'Corporal Topham, however, immediately went out alone in spite of the blasting ammunition and enemy fire and rescued the three occupants of the carrier. He brought these men back across the open, and although one died almost immediately afterwards, he arranged for the evacuation of the other two who undoubtedly owe their lives to him.'

Para, 9 Para, and some engineers and a field ambulance. As they landed the Paras went straight into action to secure the DZ and clear the enemy from surrounding woodland. The Canadians suffered casualties from enemy fire as they landed, losing their commanding officer, Lieutenant Colonel Jeff Nicklin, whose parachute caught in a tree. He was shot before he could be freed. C Company lost its commander, who was injured, and his second in command, who was killed, but two sergeants took over and cleared the enemy out of the immediate vicinity. This shows how training told: each man was ready to act on his own initiative if he had no leader. 12 Para were under orders from their commander, Lieutenant Colonel Kenneth Darling, that as soon as 20 men had assembled they were to band together under the senior person (officer or NCO) present and rush to secure their objectives. Similar tactics on a smaller scale were later used at Suez.

The glider-borne troops began to arrive at 11.00 hours, together with vehicles and guns. Some brisk fighting went on all day, and many prisoners were taken. One six-man group returned from a patrol with nearly 100 'in the bag'. 9 Para, the last of the 3rd Brigade to jump, had the easiest time: they met only light opposition and soon captured their objective, the Schneppenberg, a hill-top feature.

LYING IN WAIT

5th Parachute Brigade and their commander, Brigadier Nigel Poett, landed on a very open drop-zone under enemy fire. It took a little while to assemble everyone, and to find out where the German shooting was coming from. In Poett's own words: 'Once enemy positions had been located and action taken to deal with them, the troops in them generally surrendered without putting up a serious fight.'

7 Para, under the redoubtable Lieutenant Colonel Pine-Coffin, suffered heavy casualties while covering for 12 Para and 13 Para, who were sent to capture a strategic road and thus hamper enemy movements. But they held on. Pine-Coffin sent a platoon led by a Canadian, Lieutenant Patterson, to capture and hold an important rail and road junction. The platoon had to withstand a number of enemy attacks, but Lieutenant Patterson evolved an unorthodox method of dealing with them. If the enemy approached in force, the platoon would quietly abandon its position, move to one side and wait. When the enemy attacked the empty position, the platoon counter-attacked from the flank, inflicting heavy casualties on the Germans and taking prisoners.

BACON AND EGGS

13 Para landed on a DZ covered with dust, haze, and smoke. It was quickly in action, officers and men putting on their red berets instead of steel helmets in order 'to put the fear of God into the Germans' (commanding officer's orders), and yelling their heads off to reinforce the fear. Major Jack Watson, commanding A Company, said the Germans 'put up a resistance for the first few hours, but once they could see it was the "Red Devils", as they called us, they started to give up.'

All the commanding officers carried hunting horns to rally their men, each commander using a different call. In short order they carried all their objectives, including a farm.

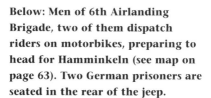

Below: Men of 6th Airlanding Brigade, two of them dispatch riders on motorbikes, preparing to head for Hamminkeln (see map on page 63). Two German prisoners are seated in the rear of the jeep.

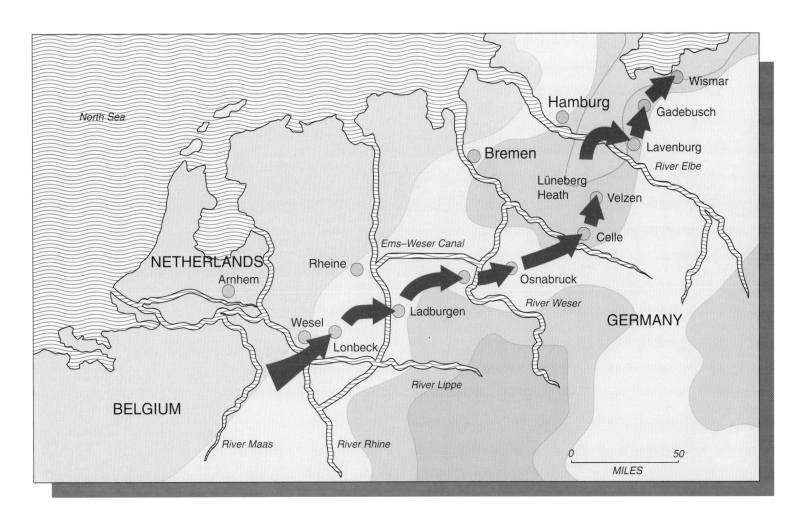

Above: The advance to the Baltic, 26 March–2 May 1945. The arrows show the troop movements. In the advance 6th Airborne were attached to 8th Corps, which was part of the British 2nd Army, but returned to the 8th US Air Corps as they crossed the Elbe.

Major Jack Watson, commanding A Company, established his company at the farm, which had been earmarked to serve as divisional headquarters. Soon Major Watson was joined by the battalion commander, Lieutenant Colonel Peter Luard, and Major General Eric Bols. Watson invited the other two commanders for breakfast, and his batman cooked eggs and bacon.

ON TO THE BALTIC

When 6th Airborne reached the River Issel they ceased to be part of Ridgeway's 8th US Airborne Corps, and were transferred to British 8th Corps, which was part of General Dempsey's 2nd Army. They had some transport, though not enough for all of them, and much of the advance had to be on foot. The brigades took it in turn to lead. They passed through and cleared a series of small towns and villages, fighting all the way. In eight days they had advanced all the way to the River Weser, a distance of 240 km (158 miles). The river was about 90 m (100 yards) wide, flowing fast, and the bridges had been destroyed. The 3rd Parachute Brigade, which was then leading, crossed by swimming or on improvised rafts.

The Airlanding Brigade were also there, and their engineers built a Bailey bridge capable of carrying heavy tanks. Bailey bridges, named after their inventor, Sir Donald Bailey, were constructed from prefabricated units which could be readily transported.

The next major river was the Leine, a tributary of the Weser. 12 Para were travelling with a Guards tank battalion, riding either on the tanks or in troop carriers. As they came in sight of the river at Bordenau, they saw the bridge over it still standing, but with what looked like a German demolition party about to destroy it. The British troops raced up to the bridge, firing with every weapon they could, and the Germans fled. The tanks gave chase over the bridge, while C Company and the battalion commander, Lieutenant Colonel Darling, stopped to remove the demolition firing wires, which they could plainly see.

B Company of 7 Para was not so lucky. They found another intact bridge over the Leine at Neustadt, but as the leading platoon was halfway across the Germans blew up the bridge, and 22 Paras died. However, Captain E. G. Woodman, Lieutenant G. B. Bush, and two soldiers, who had all run across just before the bridge went up, established a bridgehead.

RACE TO WISMAR

By 23 April the whole of 8th Corps, including the Paras, had reached the River Elbe. This was a major obstacle, being 275 m (300 yards) wide and covered by enemy artillery. It was decided to use the Paras to drop on the farther bank and establish a bridgehead, but the Germans withdrew, and the corps crossed on 29 April by boat and raft.

At this point 6th Airborne came under the control of 8th US Air Corps again. During a briefing session of 3 Para on the evening of 30 April, General Matthew Ridgeway walked in. He was a large man, and he looked particularly alarming on this occasion because he had a grenade attached to each of his shoulder straps. In his usual quiet tones he

said: 'Gentlemen, you have to be at Wismar [a port on the Baltic coast] before the Russians, to stop them getting into Denmark.' The British and Americans were anxious to limit the Soviet Union's sphere of influence to eastern Europe.

The Paras were given 12 hours to reach Wismar, riding in trucks with an armoured escort of the Royal Scots Greys. The 5th Brigade was told to lead. But Hill wanted his 3rd Brigade to get there first. The two brigades advanced on parallel roads, often hampered by columns of refugees. Hill's team won, the

Above: Brigadier James Hill (in front passenger seat) and Major General Eric Bols (driving). Behind them are a signaller and Bols' batman.

Below: A Buffalo LVPT amphibious armoured personnel carrier surges across the Rhine, ferrying troops. The men of 3rd Parachute Brigade did not have the luxury of such a craft to help them cross the fast-flowing Weser. They improvised with rafts and their ability as strong swimmers.

advance party reaching the town at 09.00 hours on 2 May. The rest of the brigade were there by midday.

Hill then sent Lieutenant Colonel Napier Crookenden, the commanding officer of 9 Para, accompanied by two Russian-speaking sergeants, to make contact with the advancing Russians. Crookenden soon met the first Russian tanks and began negotiations with the senior officer, only to see a column of Russian tanks bristling with soldiers rumble past heading for Wismar. Crookenden took off in pursuit, accompanied by the Russian officer.

After a film-style chase he overtook them, with the Russian officer panicking beside him. The Russians had set up a road block, complete with anti-tank guns. The Russian was taken to Major General Bols, and explained that his orders were to press on to Lübeck. To this Major General Bols replied that his orders were to stay put. After much argument Major General Bols said to his interpreter: 'Tell this bugger that I have a complete airborne division and five regiments of guns. If he doesn't clear off I shall open fire.' The Russian officer broke into a broad grin, and complied. But relations with the Russians remained difficult for some time.

THE END

The end of World War II in Europe came rapidly. Field Marshal Montgomery set up his headquarters on Lüneberg Heath, between the Aller and Elbe rivers. There, on 4 May, he received the formal surrender, as from the next morning, of all German forces in the Netherlands, north-west Germany, and Denmark. Hitler had already committed suicide. The capitulation of all German forces was signed at Eisenhower's HQ in Rheims, in north-east France, on 7 May, and the war officially ended on the night of 8–9 May 1945.

Below: German forces surrendering in the main square at Weimar, central Germany, May 1945. Weimar was the farthest point reached by the Paras before the war ended.

GOING EAST 1945–46

Despite the German surrender, there were 'mopping up' operations to be done in Europe. 1st Airborne Division was sent to Norway to oversee the repatriation of German forces there. 6th Airborne went home for a much-needed rest, but it was not to last long.

Brigadier Nigel Poett was salmon fishing on the River Tweed when he was summoned back to divisional headquarters. There he learned that 5th Parachute Brigade was to go to South-East Asia. Soon he was flying with Major General Bols and two members of his staff to Ceylon (now Sri Lanka), headquarters of the Supreme Allied Commander, Admiral Lord Louis Mountbatten. There they were briefed by an old friend, Lieutenant General 'Boy' Browning, who was Mountbatten's newly appointed chief of staff.

OPERATION ZIPPER

The Paras were needed for Operation Zipper, which was to free the entire Malay Peninsula from the Japanese. It soon became apparent that only one brigade group, Poett's, would be needed. The Paras' task would be to land on the causeway linking mainland Malaya with Singapore. In July the 5th Parachute Brigade group – consisting of 7 Para, 12 Para, 17 Para, 22nd Independent Parachute Company, plus an anti-tank battery, an observation unit, engineers, and a field ambulance unit – arrived in Bombay (now Mumbai), India and began training for warfare in unfamiliar terrain.

ZIPPER UNZIPPED

Driving the Japanese out of the lands they had conquered would be a bloody business, costing many lives. But on 6 August 1945, an American bomber dropped the first atomic bomb used in warfare on the Japanese city of Hiroshima, killing about 100,000 people. The Japanese government made no response, so on 9 August a second atomic bomb was dropped on Nagasaki, killing at least 40,000 people. At this the Japanese emperor, Hirohito, urged his government to give in, and three days later they agreed, formally surrendering on 2 September.

Operation Zipper was virtually unzipped; 7 Para and 12 Para did land in Malaya, but in the P & O liner Chitral. They transferred to landing craft, which left them to wade the last few yards ashore

Below: A jungle camp of 9 Para in Indonesia. A new enemy presented himself after the surrender of the Japanese – Indonesian terrorists intent on capitalizing on the post-war chaos. Ten years later the expertise of the Paras would again be called upon – see page 77.

through thick mud. After just one night they learned that their services were not required, and moved on, by way of the mud, the landing craft, and Chitral, to Singapore. The whole brigade stayed there until December, helping to restore order and train a new police force, the Japanese having disbanded the existing one.

INDONESIA

After Singapore the Brigade sailed to Batavia (now Djakarta) in Indonesia. That multi-island country had been a Dutch colony, the Dutch East Indies. The Indonesians disliked the Dutch, and had welcomed the Japanese whose advent seemed to promise them independence. When the war ended the Japanese surrendered not to the Dutch but to the Indonesians, who took their weapons. The situation was chaotic. Armed gangs roamed the cities and countryside, killing and looting, and there were large numbers of Japanese prisoners of war and civilian internees to deal with. Units of the Indian Army were struggling to restore order.

The Paras cleaned up Batavia, then they moved to the port of Semarang, where the situation was even more chaotic. The terrorists had cut off the water and electricity supplies, and there was no form of local government. Murder, arson, and looting were the order of the day. Dutch, British, and Eurasian civilians were rounded up and imprisoned. The terrorists made the mistake of murdering some of the Japanese who had officially surrendered. There was a full battalion of the Japanese, whose commander, Major Kito, realized that he would have to restore order. He marched his forces out of their barracks at one end of the town and

steadily worked his way to the centre.

Meanwhile, a Gurkha battalion had landed at the other end of the town and was also working its way to the centre. The two forces clashed, but soon realized that they were fighting a common enemy, and united under the Gurkhas' commander, Lieutenant Colonel Dick Edwards. The Paras arrived on 9 January 1946, and took over. A rumour had preceded them that they were all convicts who had been released from long prison terms on condition that they became parachutists. The terrorists regarded them with great respect!

The Paras quickly restored order, working with the Japanese and with Dutch civilians. The Royal Engineers repaired the water and electricity supplies, mended bridges and roads, and overhauled the railway. The Paras were able to hand over a peaceful town to the Dutch Army before leaving, taking the Japanese with them for repatriation.

Above: Paras about to tuck in at a field kitchen set up outside the notorious Chengi jail in Singapore, 1946. In the aftermath of the Japanese surrender the Paras helped to restore order in the region and to train a police force.

NEW GOALS, NEW ROLES

Britain ended the war with a huge army, and it was necessary to demobilize a great proportion of it as quickly as possible in order to return men to their normal occupations. The airborne forces were radically reorganized: many familiar and famous units were renamed, amalgamated, even disbanded.

Only one division was now needed, and it was decided to disband the 1st Airborne Division, and retain the 6th, now consisting of the 2nd and 3rd Parachute Brigades, and 6th Airlanding Brigade. The Canadian battalion which had been in the 3rd Brigade went home, and its place was taken by 3 Para. Several of the battalions were

disbanded, among them 12 Para and 13 Para. The end was quick and simple. Major John Sim described the ending of 12 Para: 'We paraded with all our kit. There were trucks lined up and the order was given: "12 Para to your vehicles, dismiss!" That was it.' Sim transferred to 3 Para.

Over the next 40 years there were several more reorganizations of the armed forces, culminating in the massive changes, called 'Options for Peace', which followed the break-up of the Soviet Union in December 1991. In 1997 the Parachute Regiment consisted of just three brigades. The need for parachutists to 'leap into action' is greatly reduced these days, and the Paras are generally deployed as infantry, but infantry of a particularly high calibre, as is shown by their performances in Northern Ireland and in the Falkland Islands campaign.

POST-WAR HOTSPOTS

Below: The Paras found themselves involved in less straightforward types of armed conflict after 1945, in the main against nationalist groups who wanted an end to colonial rule. Here Paras are disembarking from a troop ship at Port Said in the Canal Zone, 1950.

PALESTINE

Palestine had been under British administration, though not as a colony, ever since World War I. The main population was Arab, but over the years thousands of Jews had been allowed into what they regarded as the 'land of their fathers'. The British had limited this immigration, and the Jews in Palestine had begun a campaign of violence to persuade them to lift the restrictions.

The 6th Airborne Division arrived to help keep the peace between Jews and Arabs, only to find the Jews calling them 'Gestapo'. One of the Paras' doctors who had seen the horrors of the Nazi concentration camps was disgusted at what he saw, and commented that the Jews in Palestine were behaving 'just like Nazis'.

The Jews had four paramilitary forces. Hagana was in effect a Jewish national army, with a core of full-time soldiers called the Palmach. The other two were terrorist gangs: Irgun Zvai Laumi (IZL, or National Military Organization), and the Fighters for the Freedom of Israel (FFI, also called the Stern Gang after their founder, Abraham Stern). The Paras found themselves between these groups on the one hand and the less well-organized but volatile Arabs on the other.

The two terrorist gangs carried out repeated acts of sabotage. IZL captured, tortured, and executed several British soldiers (not Paras), whom they described as 'criminals who belong to the Nazi-British army of occupation'. Clashes between Arabs and Jews escalated into pitched battles with mortars, heavy machine-guns, and bombs. The Jews also pioneered the use of the car bomb.

It was with great relief that the Paras were withdrawn in 1948 when Palestine was partitioned and the new State of Israel was created.

CYPRUS

In January 1956 1 Para and 3 Para were flown to the then British colony of Cyprus at short notice, to be ready if it should prove necessary to evacuate British nationals from Jordan.

This turned out to be a needless scare, but the Paras were soon employed in coping with terrorists in Cyprus itself. About 80 per cent of the people of Cyprus are Greek, and the rest are Turkish. At that time the Greek Cypriots were calling for Enosis – union with Greece – and a terrorist organization called EOKA, headed by Colonel George Grivas, was carrying out acts of violence in pursuit of this aim.

The first task of the Paras was to arrest Archbishop Mihail Makarios, the head of the Greek Orthodox Church in Cyprus, who was suspected of supporting EOKA. He was exiled. The Paras spent most of their time patrolling in the hope of capturing terrorists, much of the time in the inhospitable Troodos Mountains. They almost caught Grivas in the Paphos Forest. A few days later a forest fire – reportedly started by Grivas – trapped some Army vehicles, and 32 men died.

1 Para made a brief return visit to Cyprus in 1964 to try to keep the peace between Greeks and Turks. The battalion supervised the evacuation of a number of British civilians who were living or working there.

SUEZ

In July 1956 President Gamal Abdel Nasser of Egypt nationalized the Suez Canal, then jointly owned and controlled by Britain and France. He refused to allow international use of the waterway. At this Israel, fearing an Egyptian invasion, launched a pre-emptive strike. Israel and Egypt both ignored British and French calls to withdraw from the canal zone. Britain and France at once invaded Egypt. The operation involved British and French Paras capturing airfields

at Suez. 3 Para dropped on to Gamil Airfield, near the coast, on 5 November. As the men landed they formed groups of four and dashed off to capture their objectives, the speed of the operation amazing the Egyptian defenders. In short order 3 Para cleared the airfield, captured a large amount of small arms, killed some of the opposition, and took 17 prisoners. Their own casualties were four dead and 36 wounded.

2 Para were landed by sea, and were engaged in mopping-up operations and an advance on the canal when American pressure forced the British prime minister, Anthony Eden, to halt the attack. The Paras were evacuated back to Cyprus. A military success had turned into a political defeat.

ADEN

In 1964 the southern part of Yemen formed the Aden Protectorates, which were under British rule; the port of Aden was a colony. About 80 km (50 miles) north of Aden is the Radfan, a rugged mountainous area, where local ethnic groups live in fortified houses, constantly squabbling among themselves. The main ethnic group, the Quteibi, who were backed by

Above: Paras on patrol towards the end of their tour of duty in Palestine, in 1948. All British troops who served there were under orders to shoot only if they were fired upon, which they frequently were, by both Arab and Jewish terrorist groups.

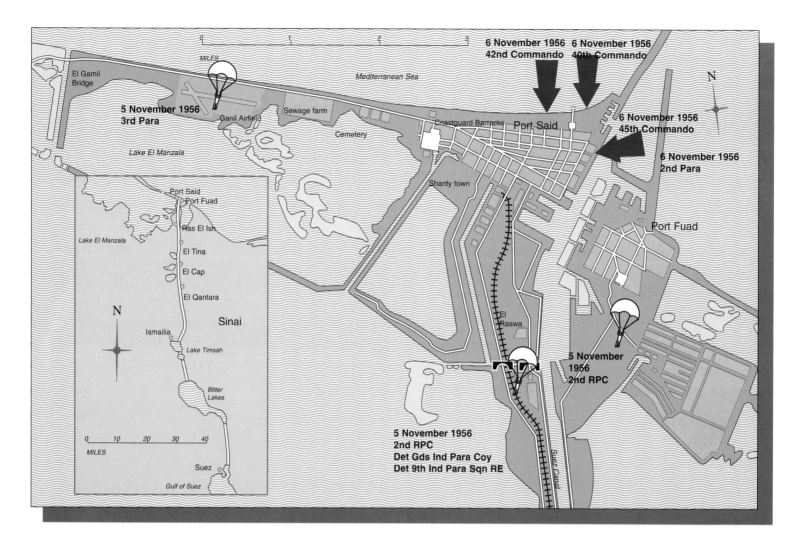

Above: The Suez campaign, November 1956. The map above shows the dropping and landing zones of the various Anglo-French forces involved in the invasion. 3 Para were in the forefront of the attack, dropping on Gamil Airfield. 2 Para were landed by sea a day later, alongside 45 Commando.

Egypt, started a rebellion. Britain sent in a tough force of peacekeepers, which included Royal Marine Commandos, a squadron of the SAS, and B Company of 3 Para.

It was a messy campaign, with an enemy whose snipers roamed freely over country they knew well. The Paras had to move carefully from one patch of cover to the next, usually under fire. On one occasion they captured a small fort which had been sheltering snipers. The only prisoner was a small and somewhat bedraggled chicken: the snipers had melted away when the Paras attacked.

On another occasion a sergeant and two soldiers were hit by enemy fire. Captain Barry Jewkes, commanding B Company, dragged them to safety, but was himself killed.

After two months the Paras were withdrawn.

The Paras were busy in Aden in 1966 and 1967, tangling with two political factions, the Front for the Liberation of Southern Yemen (FLOSY) and the National Liberation Front (NFL). Both groups were hostile to the British and to each other. Activities became particularly lively in the early weeks of 1967, in the run-up to the British withdrawal from Aden. 1 Para, commanded by Lieutenant Colonel Mike Walsh, was deputed to take control of an Arab town called Sheik Othman.

Lieutenant Colonel Walsh and his second in command, Major Joe Walsh, began by reconnoitring the town disguised as two private soldiers in a patrol of the Royal Anglian

Regiment. They made their plans from what they saw, and took over the town and its smaller neighbour, Al Mansoura, on 25 May. The minaret of a mosque in the centre of Sheik Othman was a favourite site for snipers. On 1 June the Paras came under continuous fire, with orders to the insurgents coming from someone using a loud hailer in the mosque.

Sporadic fighting continued through June to September, with Yemenis attacking the Paras with mortars, rocket launchers, and automatic weapons. The Paras' observation posts were constantly under attack.

A favourite target was the tower of the police station. This was eventually protected by a wire screen shaped like a square mushroom, which was lowered over it by helicopter. The brainchild of Major Starling, it deflected many of the missiles fired against the tower, and detonated the fuses of the rockets before they hit the building. The Paras were finally evacuated on 29 November.

OTHER OPERATIONS

The Paras had special duties in several other trouble spots in the 1960s and 1970s. In the early 1960s President Sukarno was trying to shape a Greater Indonesia by bringing together the independent countries of Malaya and Singapore, the independent Sultanate of Brunei (on the island of Borneo), and the British colonies of Sabah and Sarawak. In 1963 the three countries and two colonies formed a new country, Malaysia, to thwart Indonesian ambitions.

British troops, including Paras and SAS, were deployed to guard Brunei and the Malaysian part of Borneo against incursions from Indonesian Borneo. The Gurkha Independent Parachute Company was formed to help. The men patrolled the rain-soaked forests from their bases in jungle forts, and had several brisk fire-fights with Indonesian soldiers. The campaign lasted until 1966, when Sukarno was stripped of all except ceremonial powers.

In 1965–66 3 Para served for four months in British Guiana, which was about to become independent as Guyana. Their task was to keep the peace between the various ethnic groups there.

Another trouble spot was the Caribbean island of Anguilla, where rebels were protesting against federation with nearby St Christopher and Nevis. 2 Para was sent to restore order, but this task was in fact carried out by 120 officers of the London Metropolitan police force, who flew out with the Paras.

Below: Jungle transport in Malaya. The Paras were deployed to guard Brunei and the Malaysian part of Borneo against incursions from the troops of Indonesia's President Sukarno.

THE FALKLANDS, 1982

The background to the Paras' most famous campaign since World War II is simple. The rain-swept and windswept Falkland Islands off the coast of South America, dominated by bleak peat bogs and fells, were first sighted by Europeans in the 1500s. The first known landing was made in 1690 by an Englishman, John Strong, who named the strait between the two main islands after Viscount Falkland, then a Commissioner of the Admiralty.

The first settlers were the French in 1764. Next year Captain John Byron – known as 'Foul-weather Jack' and grandfather of the poet – claimed the islands for Britain, and left a party at Port Egmont on Saunders Island. France sold its claim to Spain for £25,000, and the Spaniards ejected the British settlers in 1770. The settlers were allowed back in 1771, but were pulled out three years later, leaving behind them a plaque saying that the islands were definitely British.

The Republic of Buenos Aires set up a colony in the islands in 1829, but a quarrel with the United States in 1831 led to a US warship laying waste the Spanish settlement and declaring the islands 'free of all governance'. In 1833 Britain resumed its occupation of the islands, which have been under British rule ever since. The population, all British by ancestry, totalled 1,200 by the 1980s. The economy was based on sheep rearing – to the extent that mutton was called 365, because the Falkland Islanders ate it every day.

Argentina, the successor state to the Republic of Buenos Aires, claimed the islands in the 1820s and called them Islas Malvinas, a corruption of Isles Malouines which Breton sailors called the islands after their home port of St Malo. And there, despite repeated Argentine claims, the matter rested until 2 April 1982.

INVASION

In December 1981 General Leopoldo Galtieri became President of Argentina. Faced with riots over the economy – inflation was galloping – Galtieri agreed to an armed invasion of the Falklands to take his people's minds off their financial plight. He believed that Britain would not bother about the Falklands. He was wrong.

On the bleak morning of 2 April 1982, the islanders woke to the sound of gunfire, and found Argentine troops pouring ashore. The only resistance was put up by the 84-strong garrison of Royal Marine Commandos. They held the invaders off for three hours, killing 15 and wounding 17, but then had to surrender.

The Argentine forces stormed the tiny capital, Port Stanley, rounded up the Marines and the Governor,

Rex Hunt, and flew them to mainland South America. Within days there were 12,000 Argentine soldiers in the Falklands, supported by aircraft, tanks, and heavy guns, with Argentine warships patrolling offshore.

The British government had been taken by surprise, but the Prime Minister, Margaret Thatcher, took immediate action. Diplomatic moves by the Americans to try to solve the crisis by peaceful means went on for days, but a task force was hurriedly assembled, beginning on the day of the Argentine invasion. 3 Para's men were on short leave; 2 Para was preparing to go to Belize, and its commander, Lieutenant Colonel H. Jones, was on a skiing holiday in Switzerland. He cut short his holiday and flew home, determined not to be left out. He was forbidden to call his

men back to base, but did so by unofficial means.

Within days a huge fleet was on its way to the South Atlantic, including besides warships the giant liners *Canberra* and *Queen Elizabeth 2*, hurriedly commandeered and converted to troopships. 3 Para travelled in *Canberra*; 2 Para, leaving a little later, in the motor-vessel *Norland*. The mid-Atlantic island of Ascension was used as a staging post for the armada. 3 Para were able to stop off for a day's training there, which including firing their weapons using training ammunition; they got through 37 years and six months' worth of their peacetime allocation of anti-tank shells.

LANDING

The opposition was fearsome. The Argentines outnumbered the British

Above: Loading stores on the Canberra at Ascension Island.

Far left: Colonel H. Jones, commanding officer of 2 Para, who won one of the two VCs awarded in the Falklands campaign. He was killed in action.

by more than two to one; they were well equipped, better fed, and had the most modern weapons. But they were badly trained and badly led. Their generals expected the attack to come at Port Stanley, in the extreme east of East Island. But the British went round into Falkland Sound and attacked by the back door at San Carlos.

D-Day was 21 May. 2 Para were in the first wave, preceded only by a reconnaissance party from the Special Boat Section. In darkness, they had to wade the last few metres because their landing craft could not get closer, and their boots stayed wet for days. 3 Para landed on a nearby beach, at dawn.

Some 5,000 men of the Paras and 3 Commando Brigade established a bridgehead at San Carlos. Overhead a fierce air battle raged. Argentine planes bombed the area. They sank the frigate HMS *Ardent* on D-Day, and over the next few days three more ships were sunk and others were damaged.

GOOSE GREEN

On 26 May Lieutenant Colonel Jones began leading 2 Para towards Darwin and Goose Green, Argentine-held settlements on an isthmus linking two halves of East Falkland. Because a large number of British helicopters had been destroyed when the ship carrying them was sunk, the Paras had to footslog it over very difficult terrain.

The attack on Darwin began early on 28 May. It was halted by heavy machine-gun fire from slit trenches on Darwin Hill, a strongpoint barring the way to the settlement. Jones led a charge to outflank the machine-gun nests in the slit trenches, but was cut down by fire from another

Above: Men of 3 Para training aboard the troop ship *Canberra* during the almost 13,000-km (8,000-mile) voyage to the South Atlantic.

trench that he had not seen. He died before he could be evacuated; later he was awarded a posthumous Victoria Cross.

Darwin Hill was captured two hours later by a determined attack supported by heavy machine-gun fire. Further advances were hampered by heavy fire and bombing from the air. But as dusk approached heavy cloud which had covered the area cleared, and three British Harrier jump-jet aircraft roared in, attacking Goose Green with cluster bombs and cannon-fire. This additional attack broke the Argentine resistance.

SURRENDER

The following morning the Argentine garrison of Goose Green surrendered. 2 Para had lost 18 dead and 35 wounded, but captured 1,100 prisoners, several heavy guns, and two aircraft. Two British servicemen from other units were killed and 12 wounded in the action. The way was now open for an advance on Port Stanley. The town was guarded by 8,000 men, who had dug in, with the support of a much-depleted Argentine air force. Many of its planes had been shot down by fire from ground troops, including some of the Paras.

Below: A photograph produced from captured Argentinian film, showing a 35 mm anti-aircraft gun in position and ready for action.

Left: A destroyed Pucara of the Argentine Air Force at Goose Green. Fire from ground troops was sufficient to bring down many of these aircraft.

Commandos made a forced march across the alternately boggy and rocky ground towards Stanley, an operation known as 'yomping'. They were carrying heavy packs and weapons. 3 Para, equally burdened, were also marching in the same direction, taking several Argentine observation posts and many prisoners along the way. 2 Para also joined in the chase. Its acting commander, Major Chris Keeble, asked the pilot

Below: Argentine prisoners of war taken by the Paras after the battle for Goose Green.

of a Chinook helicopter to airlift them. He agreed but said he could make only two more flights before dark, and thus could take only half the battalion. The peacetime load was 40 men: the pilot was persuaded to carry 80, standing, and in this way A and B companies were ferried forward. The rest of the battalion was flown in next day.

In the advance the Paras stormed a strong enemy position on Mount Longdon, on the approach to Port Stanley. In this action Sergeant McKay of 3 Para, who had taken command of 4 Platoon when its officer was wounded, stormed a heavy machine-gun position and killed its defenders with grenades. He was killed in the action, for which he received a posthumous VC.

The Falklands War ended, after a sharp battle, at 13.30 hours on 14 June, when A company of 2 Para entered Port Stanley. 3 Para and the rest of 2 Para followed soon after. The total casualties for the Parachute Regiment were 40 killed and 82 wounded, with a further 81 sick and injured, mainly through frostbite, trench foot and broken legs.

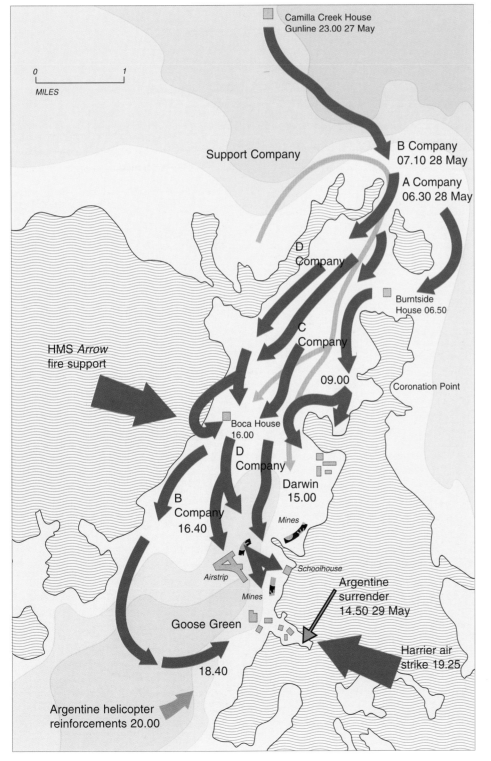

Camilla Creek House
Gunline 23.00 27 May

0   1
MILES

Support Company

B Company
07.10 28 May

A Company
06.30 28 May

D Company

Burntside
House 06.50

C Company

HMS *Arrow*
fire support

09.00

Coronation Point

Boca House
16.00

D Company

Darwin
15.00

B Company
16.40

Mines

Schoolhouse

Airstrip

Mines

Argentine
surrender
14.50 29 May

Goose Green

18.40

Harrier air
strike 19.25

Argentine helicopter
reinforcements 20.00

Left: The route taken by the Paras in the battle for Goose Green and Darwin, 28–29 May, and the support they received. No map, however, can show the difficulties of the terrain, with its many ravines – not to mention the thousands of land mines scattered by the Argentines. The troops had a cynical view of maps. One marine said: 'It's the most dangerous thing known to man – an officer with a map.'

NORTHERN IRELAND

Even to begin to understand 'The Troubles' in Northern Ireland, it must be realized that the Irish have long memories and long-lasting grudges. They also have much to hold grudges about. Back in 1155 Pope Adrian IV gave King Henry II of England the overlordship of Ireland, and authorized him to reform the Irish Church, which had never truly conformed to the Church of Rome. The fact that he had no authority to do so is beside the point.

The Norman rulers of England duly attempted to colonize Ireland, but their rule was never absolute outside an area around Dublin. The next major development came in the early 1600s, when the Stuart rulers of England began the 'Plantation of Ulster'. They confiscated the lands of two defeated Irish leaders, Hugh O'Neill, Earl of Tyrone, and Rory O'Donnell, Earl of Tyrconnell. The earls had felt their cause was hope-

less, and fled the country in 1607.

The Plantation consisted of granting estates in six of the counties of Ulster, the northernmost province of Ireland, to Protestant settlers from England and Scotland. In an island which by that time was predominantly Roman Catholic this was provocation. After the English Civil War England's Puritan ruler, Lord Protector Oliver Cromwell, made more settlements in the south. By 1680, when the monarchy had been restored in England and Scotland for twenty years, the Roman Catholic majority in Ireland owned only one-fifth of the land.

In 1688 the British deposed their Roman Catholic king, James II, and invited the very Protestant William of Orange to become king. James raised an army in Ireland, but in 1690 William defeated him at the Battle of the Boyne, a defeat still celebrated with annual marches by the

Below: A bomb explodes in Northern Ireland in 1971, as the terrorist campaign gathers momentum. On one night in July 1971 the IRA set off 20 bombs in Belfast alone, causing widespread damage.

Protestants in Northern Ireland.

During the 1800s Ireland suffered greatly as a result of a potato famine caused by disease, potatoes being then the staple diet of many of the people. Home Rule for Ireland was about to be granted when World War I broke out in 1914. Impatient at the delay, a group of Irish nationalists rebelled in 1916. The revolt failed. The Protestants of Northern Ireland wanted no part of the independence movement. A bitter guerrilla war broke out in southern Ireland, which pitted British troops against a volunteer force called the Irish Republican Army (IRA). The war ended with a treaty which gave self-government to the 26 southern counties, and left the six northern counties, by their own wish, as a province of the UK.

SINN FEIN

The leading political party in Ireland was Sinn Féin ('We Ourselves') founded in 1905, which had authorized the IRA to campaign for independence. When the 26 counties became the Republic of Ireland in 1949, the new country's constitution laid claim to the six northern counties, a claim never altered.

All might have been well if the Protestant-dominated parliament of Northern Ireland had treated the Roman Catholic minority in the Six Counties on equal terms. But they did not: there was discrimination against them in jobs, housing, and local government. In 1969 Roman Catholic protests led to riots, in which Protestant mobs attacked them. At this point the IRA, which had been quiescent for years, split: a militant breakaway section called the Provisional IRA was formed, and began using violence to try to secure

A GEORGE CROSS

In one incident in May 1971 a suitcase containing a bomb was dropped into a Belfast police station. Sergeant Willetts of 3 Para realized what it was, and shepherded people outside. Before he too could escape the bomb went off, and he was killed. As his body was carried to an ambulance a mob jeered at it, and some people spat on the stretcher. For his courage, Sergeant Willetts was awarded a posthumous George Cross.

the union of Ireland. This is where the Paras first came into the picture.

A CALL FOR HELP

In 1969 riots and terrorism were so bad that the Northern Ireland provincial government appealed for help. In October, 1 Para, commanded

Below: A soldier of 2 Para takes cover while on patrol in Belfast in 1970. From 1970 the three battalions of the Paras took it in turns to keep order in the Province, usually on four-month tours of duty.

by Lieutenant Colonel Michael Gray, was sent to Ulster to try to restore order. At first Protestants and Roman Catholics both greeted the peace-keepers with relief, but soon the Catholics began to regard them as supporting the Protestants against them. But by February 1970, when 1 Para completed its tour of duty, it had the confidence of both sides.

The situation deteriorated, and Provisional IRA gunmen (known as the 'Provos') fired on the soldiers who were trying to keep the peace, and threw grenades at them. From then on the three battalions of the Paras took it in turn to perform the task of trying to keep order in Northern Ireland. They were usually on four-month tours of duty.

BLOODY SUNDAY

On Sunday, 30 January 1972, 1 Para, now commanded by Lieutenant Colonel Derek Wilford, was trying to keep order during a Catholic protest march in Londonderry. The march had been declared illegal, but its organizers went ahead with it. The march included a large number of young men who threw bricks, stones, and tear-gas bombs at the soldiers. Then somebody fired a shot at the Paras. A moment later one of the rioters was seen to be igniting a nail bomb. Two Paras shot him dead before he could throw it.

A little later the Paras came under machine-gun fire. Both gunmen were shot dead, as were three others who opened fire. Some Provos were throwing bottles of acid, and the crowd was panicking. All this time the Paras were trying to arrest the trouble-makers. In the gun battle a total of 13 young men were shot dead, while more than 40 rioters were arrested. The Provos claimed that the soldiers fired indiscriminately on unarmed civilians, but the fact that no older men, or women and children, of which there were many in the crowd, were hit shows that the firing was not indiscriminate. Provo propaganda resulted in the incident passing into legend as 'Bloody Sunday'.

A judicial inquiry into the incident concluded that the soldiers only opened fire after they had been shot at, and were following standing instructions. But it did say that some of the Paras had been 'reckless'. In 1997 new evidence suggested that recklessness had indeed been to the fore.

BLOODY FRIDAY

Violence continued through 1971 and 1972. On one night in July 1971 terrorists set off 20 bombs in Belfast, causing widespread damage. A few weeks later, when mobs were roaming the streets setting fire to buildings and hijacking buses, 2 Para and a company from 1 Para took part in a 'search and arrest' operation, in which a number of suspects were arrested and taken away for internment without trial – a move that was very unpopular with the terrorists. Internment was later suspended.

Altogether in 1971 the British Army lost more than 40 men as a result of action by the Provos. The terror campaign reached its height in 1972, with the Provos carrying out daily bombings. On Friday 21 July that year the Provos carried out 19 bomb attacks in Belfast in 65 minutes, killing nine people and seriously wounding 130. That episode became known as 'Bloody Friday'.

At that time there were 'no go' areas in Roman Catholic parts of

Above: Paras with a cache of terrorist weapons found in Belfast in 1976.

Belfast and Londonderry, where it was not safe for police, troops, or Protestants to venture, and the authorities decided that it was time to clean them up. In Operation Motorman 21,000 troops were deployed, including 2 Para. As a result the terrorists who had dominated the areas fled, and relative peace returned to them, apart from occasional sniping at the troops.

WARRENPOINT

The terror attacks in Northern Ireland waxed and waned. A notable one involving 2 Para occurred on 29 August 1979. A convoy consisting of a Land Rover and two four-ton trucks carrying men of A Company was driving along a road near the village of Warrenpoint, on the shores of Carlingford Lough, a sea inlet that forms the boundary between Northern Ireland and the Republic of Ireland. Warrenpoint is near the head of the lough, which at that point is only about 180 m (200 yards) wide.

Near Narrow Water Castle, a medieval ruin, there was a lay-by in which was a parked trailer loaded with straw. As the convoy passed the trailer a group of Provos lying in wait on the republic side of the lough set off by radio control a 227-kg (500-lb) bomb hidden in the trailer. The bomb destroyed one of the trucks, setting it on fire, and killed six Paras.

The rest of the convoy stopped and the Paras in the trucks ran back to help their comrades. At this the Provos opened fire from across the lough. The Paras returned the fire. Ammunition in the burning truck began to explode. Meanwhile a Royal Marine patrol had heard the explosion and radioed for help. Reinforcements from the Paras, with

A Company's commander, Major Peter Fursman, rushed to the scene in Land Rovers, and an airborne reaction force from the Queen's Own Highlanders arrived by helicopter with medical help.

Major Fursman and some of the Paras took cover at a gatehouse nearby. Soon afterwards, another helicopter arrived with the Highlanders' own commander, Lieutenant Colonel David Blair, who ran over to the gatehouse. But the Provos, who had earmarked the gatehouse area as a likely rallying point, detonated a second bomb, twice the size of the first, which they had hidden in the gateway. Lieutenant Colonel Blair caught the full force of the blast, and his body was vaporized; all that was found of him was one of his rank badges. The blast killed Major Fursman and ten other men, and slightly damaged one of the helicopters which was just taking off laden with wounded. This attack was typical of what the Paras have endured in the province, where the ceasefire in 1994–95 was the only period of peace in 25 years of violence.

Below: A joint Army and Royal Ulster Constabulary patrol in Bessbrook, 1978.

WHAT NEXT?

Opposite: A Pathfinder from 5th Airborne Brigade on exercise on Salisbury Plain. He is armed with an M16A2 5.56 mm rifle fitted with M203 launcher.

Below: Paras boarding a C130 Hercules transporter.

In spite of the ending of the Cold War, it is all too certain that there will be a need for Britain's armed forces for many years to come. And specialist units such as the Parachute Regiment, with their exceptionally high training and skills, will always be in the forefront of the army of the 21st century.

As currently (1997) established, the Parachute Regiment consists of three battalions, each of about 600 officers and other ranks. In each battalion there are three rifle companies, a patrol company, a fire support company, and a headquarters company. The battalion includes a number of specialists – snipers, signallers, machine-gunners, and soldiers operating anti-tank guns and mortars. The headquarters includes medical staff and transport.

But the main element of the Paras is that the men are all trained to do several jobs, and to work closely with each other and take on other roles when casualties put colleagues out of action. As one retired Para told me, what he had learned in serving in the Regiment had stood him in good stead in dealing with the problems of civilian life.

The men learn to rely on each other and on themselves. Not for nothing is the motto of the Regiment the same as that of the Three Musketeers: 'Ad Unum Omnes' – 'All For One'.

Opposite: It's a hard slog in the log race. Here a group of eight P Company hopefuls are put through their paces. The log is in fact a telegraph pole which the men have to run with for 16 km (10 miles) as part of the initial physical endurance test that has to be passed.

Above: Training with the Wombat 120 mm anti-tank gun, the standard gun of this type in the British Army for over 30 years.

Left: An instructor shows a novice how to lay a booby-trap during training at the battle school, Brecon. Here the device is a pyrotechnic flare attached to a trip wire.

Left: A Para wearing full jump order. He has his main and reserve parachutes, a life preserver, his Bergen pack on quick-release straps below his reserve, and a LAW 80 weapon strapped to its side.

Right: Range training with the SA80, the standard British Army infantry small arm, at the battle school, Brecon.

Left: All the comforts of home. A Para prepares a fry up while on a training exercise. Self-sufficiency is a key component of the Paras' training. The four-week pre-Para course that every aspiring candidate has to endure is extremely demanding and unique to the Regiment. Successful candidates who go on to be accepted into the Regiment need never complete the whole course again. However, parts of the course are used in the Paras' ongoing training regime.

Right: Paras scaling the 3.5-metre (12-foot) wall, one of the elements in the basic British Army infantry assault course which the Paras use – together with their own specialist training programmes – to keep themselves in peak physical condition.

Left: P Company swap the log for a stretcher, on the last leg of their physical endurance course. The 'stretcher' is made out of scaffolding and metal tank plates (sand channels) and is the equivalent in weight of a 95-kg (15-stone) man.

INDEX